500 RECIPES FOR SOUPS AND SAVOURIES

Savoury supper snacks on our cover: Stuffed peppers (page 39);
Quick pizzas (page 88); Stuffed mushrooms (cocktail snack version
page 55); Sausage croquette with apple ring (page 69); Savoury choux
with ham and shrimp fillings (pages 48–49); Liver pâté (page 41). For
French onion soup see page 20.

Photograph: Roy Rich

500 RECIPES FOR SOUPS AND SAVOURIES

by Marguerite Patten

HAMLYN

LONDON · NEW YORK · SYDNEY · TORONTO

Contents

Published by
The Hamlyn Publishing Group Limited
London · New York · Sydney · Toronto
Hamlyn House, Feltham, Middlesex, England
© Copyright The Hamlyn Publishing Group Limited 1964
Fourth impression 1972

ISBN 0 600 03425 9

Printed in England by Index Printers, Dunstable, Bedfordshire

Introduction

In these busy days when so many housewives go out to work and main meals are often eaten out by husbands, children and the working mother, it is often considered sufficient to have a sustaining savoury at night. You will find in this book a large variety of savouries that form the basis of a meal.

There are, however, other savoury dishes that add interest to more elaborate meals:

- hors-d'oeuvre which can turn a family meal into one for a special occasion;
- savouries which can be served at the end of a meal, either in place of a sweet or after a sweet (there are chapters covering both types of dishes);

- cocktail party savouries—most people choose all savoury dishes to serve with drinks, many of them possible to prepare in a few moments, and you will find a number of ideas for this type of recipe.

In spite of the excellent variety of ready-prepared soups on the market there are many occasions when a housewife would like to make her own and the section of this book devoted to soups gives many basic recipes that can be varied according to the foods available or in season.

This is a book for practical housewives who desire variety in food without spending too much time on preparation.

Some Useful Facts and Figures

Comparison of Weights and Measures

English weights and measures have been used throughout the book. 3 teaspoonfuls equal 1 tablespoon. The average English teacup is $\frac{1}{4}$ pint. The average English breakfast cup is $\frac{1}{2}$ pint. When cups are mentioned in recipes they refer to a B.S.I. measuring cup which holds $\frac{1}{2}$ pint or 10 fluid ounces. In case it is wished to translate quantities into American of metric counterparts the following give a comparison.

Liquid measure

The American pint is 16 fluid ounces, as opposed to the British Imperial pint and Canadian pint which are 20 fluid ounces. The American $\frac{1}{2}$-pint measuring cup is therefore equivalent to $\frac{2}{5}$ British pint. In Australia the British Imperial pint, 20 fluid ounces, is used.

Solid measure

British	American
1 lb. butter or other fat	2 cups
1 lb. flour	4 cups
1 lb. granulated or castor sugar	2 cups
1 lb. sifted icing or confectioners' sugar	$3\frac{1}{2}$ cups

British	American
1 lb. brown (moist) sugar (firmly packed)	2 cups
12 oz. golden syrup or treacle	1 cup
14 oz. rice	2 cups
1 lb. dried fruit	3 cups
1 lb. chopped or minced meat (firmly packed)	2 cups
1 lb. lentils or split peas	2 cups
2 oz. soft breadcrumbs	1 cup
$\frac{1}{2}$ oz. flour	2 tablespoons
1 oz. flour	$\frac{1}{4}$ cup
1 oz. sugar	2 tablespoons
$\frac{1}{2}$ oz. butter	1 tablespoon
1 oz. golden syrup or treacle	1 tablespoon
1 oz. jam or jelly	1 tablespoon
All U.S. standard measuring cups and tablespoons	

To help you understand metrication

You will see from the chart that 1 oz. is approximately 28 g. but can be rounded off to the more convenient measuring unit of 25. Also the figures in the right hand column are not always increased by 25. This is to reduce the difference between the convenient number and the nearest equivalent.

The conversion chart

Ounces/fluid ounces	Approx. g. and ml. to nearest whole number	Recommended nearest unit of 25
1	28	25
2	57	50
3	85	75
4	113	125
5 (¼ pint)	142	150
6	170	175
7	198	200
8 (½ lb.)	226	225
9	255	250
10 (½ pint)	283	275
12 (¾ lb.)	340	350
15 (¾ pint)	428	425
16 (1 lb.)	456	450
20 (1 pint)	569	575

Note: When converting quantities over 20 oz. first add the appropriate figures in the centre column, not those given in the right hand column, THEN adjust to the nearest unit of 25. It may be useful to note that 1 litre (1000 millilitres, 10 decilitres) equals 1·76 pints, or almost exactly 1¾ pints; 1 kilogramme (1000 grammes) equals 2·2 pounds, or almost exactly 2 lb. 3 oz.

Oven temperatures

The chart below gives conversions from degrees Fahrenheit to degrees Celcius recommended by manufacturers of electric cookers.

Description	°F.	°C.	Gas Mark
very cool	225	110	¼
	250	130	½
cool	275	140	1
	300	150	2
moderate	325	170	3
	350	180	4
moderately hot	375	190	5
	400	200	6
hot	425	220	7
	450	230	8
very hot	475	240	9

Making Your Own Soups

In this chapter you will find recipes for not only the most popular soups but also for some of the less usual ones. And don't forget that a home-made soup is not only delicious—it is also often extremely economical.

When preparing vegetable soups, take advantage of those vegetables that are in season and use them to give variety to your menus. Alternatively, often a meat bone or chicken carcase can be the basis of a really sustaining economical soup. By using the left-over bones, you need spend no further money on ingredients.

Because the ready-prepared soups are used so often by the busy housewife, you will also find a chapter on making the less usual and more interesting of these.

In soup-making there are certain terms which may need interpretation:

Bouquet garni The usual is a small bunch containing sprigs of parsley and thyme, and a bayleaf. You may also add 1–2 chives and any less usual herbs such as rosemary, marjoram, sage or fresh mint. The herbs are put into the stock (tied securely with cotton) and are either sieved with the other ingredients or removed before serving.

When fresh herbs are not available then use a good pinch of mixed dried herbs. Do not be too generous with dried herbs since they tend to give a musty flavour when used too lavishly.

Stock A white stock is made from the bones of chicken or veal: a brown stock from beef, mutton or game. When time does not permit using your own stock it is possible to use either yeast or beef extract or stock cubes with water.

Seasoning Whilst this normally means just salt and pepper, you will find that you can add considerable interest to soups by being rather more enterprising with seasoning—by using celery salt, garlic salt, paprika or cayenne pepper and pinches of spices from time to time.

A little white wine is often the secret of a really delicious soup. Use a light sherry or white wine for vegetable soups and a dark sherry or red wine in the rather heavier meat soups.

A soup that is sometimes lacking in richness tastes completely different if a knob of butter or tablespoon of cream is added to each portion just before serving.

Quantities to allow
It is very difficult to lay down hard and fast rules as to how much soup one should allow. If you are following the soup with a substantial main course, you generally allow ⅓ pint of a clear soup, and ¼ pint of a more filling soup. If, however, the soup is to be the most filling part of the meal, increase these quantities.

Preparing stock
Cover bones with cold water, add a bay leaf, seasoning, and simmer gently for several hours.

Brown stocks are made from beef bones, mutton and game and are used mainly for meat soups.

White stocks are made from poultry bones (but do not include any giblets or meat from the bird) and from veal. They are used mainly for vegetable soups.

Fish stocks are made from the bones and skin of fish, or the shells of fish, and are used in fish soups.

Bacon stock: when you have stock left from boiling a piece of ham or bacon use it with such soups as pea (see page 21); you'll find the flavour excellent. A lentil or vegetable soup can be made with bacon stock too, with very good results.

Vegetable stocks are made by boiling vegetables and are used for many vegetable soups.

Note:
1 A stock pot should not be left in a warm kitchen where the liquid may go off. The stock should be used soon after making or kept in a refrigerator.
2 Potatoes and green vegetables are not good things to add to stock which is not being used immediately because they cause it to deteriorate.

Stock cubes
If you find you haven't enough bones left over to use as the basis of stock, or if making stock takes up too much time, there are stock cubes on the market which give an excellent flavour to soups. They are dissolved in water, then added to the soup. You can buy both chicken and beef flavours, using the former for white stock and the latter for brown. Both yeast and beef extracts can be used for flavouring brown stock.

Cooking soups in a pressure cooker

No special recipes are given for pressure cooked soups because any recipe can be cooked this way. The time varies, of course, according to the type of ingredients but you need approximately a quarter of the amount of cooking time for most vegetables. Here are the points to remember about soup making in a pressure cooker.

Generally speaking, you will need to use approximately half the usual amount of water or stock for long-cooking soups. This is because you have little, if any, evaporation in a pressure cooker, which has been allowed for in the saucepan recipes. Where the ordinary saucepan method for soup takes only a few minutes decrease the amount of liquid by just under a third.

When making soup remember not to fill the cooker too full. You do not need the rack in the bottom of the pressure cooker.

Generally speaking soups should be cooked at a 15 lb. pressure and the pressure then allowed to return to normal at room temperature.

Where soups are sieved and thickened afterwards you will then treat the pressure cooker like an ordinary saucepan for thickening.

Using an electric blender

An electric blender or liquidiser is an admirable way of producing a purée soup without long cooking and without rubbing the ingredients through a sieve, and can be substituted whenever sieving is indicated in recipes. Vegetables and especially tomatoes, retain the maximum amount of flavour if lightly cooked, so you can produce a much better tomato soup if you purée the tomatoes in the electric mixer before cooking. Preparation of mixed vegetable soups in this way will reduce the cooking time by well under half but it has been found that onions which are cooked for such a short time tend to have a rather strong and, to some people, unpalatable flavour, so in any special recipe with a high percentage of onion it is better if ingredients are fully cooked before being put into the blender.

The parts of a blender are usually made of heat resisting materials but even so it is wise to warm them slightly for a minute or so before putting in a boiling soup.

To serve with soup

Croûtons

cooking time   few minutes

you will need:

bread   hot fat for frying

1 Cut bread into really small dice or other shapes.
2 Toast or fry in hot fat until crisp and golden brown.
3 Drain on kitchen paper.

Caraway seed toast fingers

you will need:

crusts from slices of   butter
  bread   caraway seeds

1 Butter one side of the crusts only and sprinkle with caraway seeds.
2 Toast the buttered side to a golden brown and cut into fingers.
3 Serve at once.

Melba toast

Cut wafer-thin slices of stale bread and crisp them in the oven on a moderately low heat until golden brown.

10-Minute Soups

A really nourishing soup can turn a light snack into a complete and satisfying meal and the soups in this chapter all take a maximum of 10 minutes to prepare.

Asparagus soup

cooking time   just under 10 minutes

you will need for 4 servings:

1 medium can asparagus   1 oz. butter or
1 pint milk   margarine
½ oz. cornflour or   extra seasoning
  1 oz. flour

1 Open the can of asparagus and drain the liquid into a jug with the milk.
2 Chop the asparagus into tiny pieces.
3 Heat the butter or margarine, stir in the cornflour or flour.
4 Add the milk and asparagus stock.
5 Bring to the boil, taste and season.
6 Put in the pieces of asparagus.
7 Heat for a few minutes and serve.

Bean broth

cooking time   under 10 minutes

you will need for 4 servings:

1 pint stock or water   1 tablespoon chopped
  with one chicken   parsley
  stock cube or little   1 tablespoon chopped
  yeast extract   chives
2 skinned, chopped   1 medium can baked
  tomatoes   beans

1 Put all the ingredients into a saucepan and simmer for approximately 5 minutes.
2 This can be served topped with grated cheese if wished.

Beetroot soup

cooking time   just under 10 minutes

you will need for 4 servings:

1 large cooked beetroot   seasoning
2 chicken or beef stock   squeeze lemon juice
  cubes
1½ pints water   **To garnish:**
                                chopped parsley

8

1 Skin the beetroot and grate.
2 Heat the water and stock cubes.
3 Add grated beetroot, lemon juice and seasoning, and heat for about 5 minutes.
4 Top with chopped parsley.

Carrot soup

cooking time   10 minutes

you will need for 4 servings:

8 small carrots	seasoning
1 pint water	
½ pint milk	**To garnish:**
1–2 chicken stock cubes	chopped parsley or chives

1 Grate the carrots and simmer for about 8
minutes with the milk and water in which the
stock cubes have been dissolved.
2 Season well and include a pinch of sugar if
wished.
3 Pour into heated soup cups and garnish with
the parsley or chives.

Variations:

Quick cream of carrot soup
Simmer the carrots with the water only. Meanwhile make a white sauce with ½ oz. butter, ½ oz.
flour and ½ pint milk. Blend with the carrot
mixture and season well.

Cheese and carrot soup
During the last 2 minutes of cooking of either
the plain carrot soup or cream of carrot soup,
stir in 4 oz. grated cheese. If overcooked it will
become tough and stringy.

Corn-on-the-cob soup

cooking time   just under 10 minutes

you will need for 4 servings:

1 oz. margarine or butter	1 can sweetcorn or mixed sweetcorn and peppers
½ oz. cornflour or 1 oz. flour	seasoning
½ pint water	
1 stock cube (preferably chicken)	**To garnish:** little chopped chives or parsley
1 pint milk	

1 Heat the butter or margarine, stir in the cornflour or flour.
2 Cook gently for several minutes.
3 Add the water, stock cube, and milk and bring
to the boil.

4 Cook until thickened.
5 Add the sweetcorn and heat for a few minutes.
6 Season well and garnish with chopped chives
or parsley.

Fish soup

cooking time   just under 10 minutes

you will need for 4 servings:

2 good-sized fillets plaice, whiting or sole	1 oz. butter or margarine
2 teaspoons grated onion	seasoning
1 pint milk	
¼ pint water	
½ oz. cornflour or 1 oz. flour	**To garnish:** lemon slices chopped parsley
¼ pint white wine or ½ pint water	

1 Skin the fish and cut into tiny pieces with a
sharp knife or kitchen scissors.
2 Simmer the fish with the onion in milk and
water for about 5 minutes.
3 Blend the cornflour or flour with the wine or
the water.
4 Add to the fish mixture.
5 Bring to the boil, stirring well.
6 Put in the butter or margarine and seasoning,
and heat for 2–3 minutes.
7 Pour into soup cups and garnish with lemon
and parsley.

Speedy green pea soup

cooking time   just under 10 minutes

you will need for 4 servings:

1 pint water	pinch dried mint or little chopped fresh mint
1 chicken stock cube	
1 small packet frozen peas or 1 can peas	approximately 3 table-spoons top of milk or cream
seasoning	

1 Bring water in which stock cube is dissolved to
the boil.
2 Put in frozen peas and cook for about 4 minutes.
Canned peas need only about 2 minutes
heating.
3 Rub through a sieve, return to the pan with the
remaining ingredients and reheat.

Variation:
To make a soup with a stronger flavour, 1 or 2
finely diced rashers of bacon can also be
cooked with the peas.

Potato soup

cooking time — just under 10 minutes

you will need for 4 servings:

4 medium potatoes
1 small onion
½ pint milk
1 pint water

1–2 chicken stock cubes
seasoning

To garnish:
chopped chives or
parsley

1 Grate the peeled potatoes and onion and simmer for about 8 minutes with the milk and water in which the stock cubes have been dissolved.
2 Season well and include a pinch of sugar if wished.
3 Pour into hot soup cups and garnish with the chives or parsley.

Variation:

Cheese and potato soup
Use either plain Potato soup or Cream of potato soup and in the last two minutes of cooking stir in 4 oz. grated cheese. Do not overcook or it will become tough and stringy.

Quick vegetable soup

cooking time — 8 minutes

you will need for 4 servings:

approximately 1¼ lb.
  mixed vegetables
1½ pints stock or water
1 bouillon cube
seasoning

To garnish:
grated cheese
parsley

1 Peel and coarsely grate the vegetables.
2 Bring to the boil the stock or water to which the bouillon cube has been added, add the vegetables and seasoning and cook rapidly for about 5–8 minutes until the vegetables are just tender.
3 Pour into hot soup cups and sprinkle with lots of grated cheese and parsley.

Fish Soups

It is a pity that people are often so reluctant to try fish soups because they can be extremely good. Their great virtue lies in the fact that one can choose quite cheap fish as a basis for family soups or more luxurious fish for party fare. They are easily digestible and make a good choice to precede a meat course.

Basic fish soup

cooking time — 55 minutes

you will need for 4 servings:

1 lb white fish*
8 oz. fish trimmings
  (skin, bones)
2 pints water
1 large onion or 2 leeks
1 oz. margarine

2 oz. flour
¼ pint milk
salt and pepper to taste
1 teaspoon chopped
  parsley

*Whiting gives a very delicately flavoured soup; fresh haddock gives a moderately strong flavour, while cod has a very definite flavour

1 Wash and clean fish and trimmings.
2 Simmer trimmings in water for 10 minutes. Strain.
3 Place fish in a pan with the stock and sliced onions or leeks. Bring to the boil and skim well. Cook gently for 10 minutes.
4 Lift out the fish and flake.
5 Cook the stock for 30 minutes longer. Strain and rinse the pan.
6 Melt the margarine, add the flour and cook without colouring for a few minutes. Add the stock and milk and cook until boiling, stirring continuously.
7 Add the flaked fish, season and boil gently for 5 minutes.
8 Add the chopped parsley and serve.

Variations:

Spiced fish soup
Add 2–3 cloves and/or a little grated nutmeg.

Brown fish soup
Use a brown meat stock. This seems a strange mixture but it is, in fact, very pleasant.

Tomato fish soup
Use either 1 pint water and 1 pint tomato juice or a thin sieved tomato purée.

Lobster bisque

cooking time   45 minutes

you will need for 4 servings:

½ large lobster or
  1 small lobster
1 pint water or fish
  stock
1 teaspoon lemon juice
1 oz. flour
½ pint milk

2 oz. margarine or
  butter
seasoning
2 tablespoons cream

To garnish:
paprika pepper
small pieces lobster

1 Remove the flesh from the lobster and cut into small pieces.
2 Put aside a few pieces for garnishing.
3 Put the shell, well washed and crushed, into a large saucepan.
4 Cover with the water or stock, add lemon juice and simmer gently for a good 30 minutes.
5 Strain carefully through a fine sieve and return liquid to the pan together with the lobster meat.
6 Blend the flour with the milk and stir this into the soup together with the margarine or butter, and season.
7 Bring slowly to the boil and cook, stirring all the time until thickened.
8 Add the cream, reheat and serve.
9 Garnish with paprika pepper and the small pieces of lobster.

Creamed haddock soup

cooking time   20 minutes

you will need for 4 servings:

1 small onion
approximately 12 oz.
  fresh haddock
small bunch parsley
½ pint water
1 oz. butter
1 oz. flour

½ pint milk
seasoning

To garnish:
a little onion or red
  pepper or paprika
  pepper

1 Slice the onion and put with the haddock and parsley into the water.
2 Simmer gently until just soft.
3 Lift the fish out of the stock and flake very finely.
4 Make a thin sauce with the butter, flour, milk and a good ¼ pint of the fish stock.
5 Add the pieces of fish and heat gently.
6 Season.
7 Garnish with wafer-thin slices of raw or fried onion, or slices of pepper, or dust instead with a little paprika to give a contrasting colour.

Mussel soup

cooking time   30 minutes

you will need for 4 servings:

2 pints mussels
1 finely chopped onion
2 tablespoons finely
  chopped celery
small bunch parsley
seasoning
2 oz. rice

1 large skinned chopped
  tomato
1½ pints water
squeeze lemon juice or
  little vinegar

To garnish:
chopped parsley

1 Scrub mussels, discarding any that are open and will not close when sharply tapped. Always remove the 'beard' (the rather stringy part).
2 Put into a large saucepan with onion, celery, parsley and seasoning and heat slowly until mussels open.
3 Remove mussels from liquid and take out of shells.
4 Meanwhile reheat liquid, add rice and cook until tender with chopped tomato.
5 Remove sprig of parsley, add mussels and lemon juice or vinegar, and reheat gently.
6 Garnish with chopped parsley.

Scallop bisque

cooking time   20–40 minutes

you will need for 4 servings:

2 tablespoons oil for
  frying
1 carrot
1 leek
1 clove garlic
pinch of fennel (optional)
4 peppercorns
8 oz. white fish

2 *level* tablespoons
  cornflour
1 small can tomato purée
¼ pint dry white wine
¼ pint water
1½ pints milk
4 scallops
3 tablespoons cream
salt

1 Heat the oil in a deep pan.
2 Chop the carrot, leek and garlic finely and add to the oil with fennel and peppercorns.
3 Sauté lightly.
4 Cut the white fish into small pieces.
5 Add to the vegetables.
6 Continue cooking gently for 2–3 minutes.
7 Add the cornflour and tomato purée.
8 Mix well, then add the wine and water.
9 Bring to the boil, then add the milk.
10 Cover, and cook gently for about 20 minutes or until the vegetables are tender.
11 Put through a sieve.
12 Cut the scallops into small pieces, add to the soup and return to gentle heat for about 10 minutes or until the scallops are tender.
13 Stir in the cream and season to taste.

Meat Soups

Bacon and barley soup

cooking time   1 hour 20 minutes

you will need for 6–8 servings:

1 bacon knuckle	1 turnip
2½ pints stock	1 onion
2 oz. pearl barley	
pepper	**To garnish:**
2 carrots	chopped parsley

1 Soak the knuckle in cold water (6 hours if smoked, 2 hours if unsmoked).
2 Place in a saucepan with the stock.
3 Wash barley and add.
4 Season with pepper and bring to the boil.
5 Reduce heat, cover with lid and simmer gently for 40 minutes.
6 Add diced carrots, turnip and onion and simmer for further 40 minutes.
7 Remove knuckle from liquid and cut meat into small pieces.
8 Return these to the soup.
9 Taste and adjust seasoning if necessary.
10 Serve garnished with chopped parsley.

Kidney soup

cooking time   1½ hours

you will need for 4 servings:

8 oz. kidney (ox kidney can be used)*	2 pints stock or water
1 small onion	seasoning
2 oz. butter	parsley
1 oz. flour	little port or Burgundy

*If using lambs' kidneys the cooking time will be 30 minutes only so reduce the amount of stock to 1¼–1½ pints

1 Chop the kidney and onion very finely and fry in the hot butter for a minute or two, making sure not to harden the outside of the meat.
2 Blend in the flour, and gradually add the stock.
3 Bring to the boil, stir until smooth, add seasoning and a sprig of parsley, then simmer gently for about 1½ hours.
4 Remove the parsley, add wine and serve.

Chinese meat and vegetable soup

cooking time   12 minutes

you will need for 4 servings:

4 oz. greens*	1 tablespoon sherry
4 oz. lean pork	1 teaspoon salt
1 pint stock	⅓ teaspoon taste powder†

*You can use spinach, celery, cabbage, peas or green beans
†Sold in good grocers' shops—monosodium glutamate

1 Wash greens and cut into 1-inch lengths.
2 Slice meat and cut into ¼-inch dice.
3 Bring stock to the boil and slide meat in.
4 Boil ½ minute, then remove meat with a strainer or sieve.
5 Holding sieve over the pot of soup, pour sherry over meat and into soup.
6 Skim soup.
7 Add greens and simmer until tender.
8 Place meat with salt and taste powder in a bowl, pour soup over and stir well.

Mulligatawny soup

cooking time   1 hour

you will need for 4 servings:

1 apple	2 pints stock*
1 large carrot	1 tablespoon chutney
2 onions	1 oz. sultanas
2 oz. fat or dripping	pinch sugar
1 oz. flour	seasoning
1 tablespoon curry powder	little lemon juice or vinegar

*Made by simmering lamb or mutton bones or a small lamb's head

1 Chop the apple and vegetables into tiny pieces, toss in the hot dripping, then work in the flour and curry powder.
2 Add the stock, bring to the boil and cook until thickened.
3 Add remaining ingredients and cook together for about 45 minutes–1 hour.
4 Rub through a sieve and return to the pan to reheat.
5 Taste, adjusting seasoning if necessary, and add a little extra sugar or lemon juice if required.

Oxtail soup

cooking time $3\frac{1}{4}$ hours

you will need for 4 servings:

1 small oxtail	1 large onion
2 oz. cooking fat or	3 pints stock or water
margarine	good pinch mixed herbs
1 small turnip	seasoning
3 medium carrots	2 oz. flour

1 Soak the cut-up oxtail for an hour or so then throw away the water.
2 Heat the fat, slice the vegetables and fry for about 5 minutes.
3 Add the stock, reserving 1 teacup, the oxtail, herbs and plenty of seasoning and simmer gently for about 3 hours.
4 Blend the flour with the teacup of cold stock or water and stir this into the soup.
5 Bring to the boil and cook for about 10 minutes.
6 Take out the pieces of oxtail, cut the meat from the bones, return to the soup and reheat.
7 As this soup will have a fair amount of fat it is best made the day before required, so that you can allow it to cool and then remove the fat from the top.

Scotch broth

cooking time $2\frac{3}{4}$ hours

you will need for 4 servings:

1 oz. pearl barley	8 oz. diced swede
8 oz. stewing beef or	salt and pepper
mutton	2 oz. sliced cabbage
2 pints water	
3 oz. sliced leeks or	**To garnish:**
onion	1 tablespoon chopped
8 oz. diced carrot	parsley

1 Blanch the barley by putting into cold water bringing to the boil, then pouring the water away.
2 Put the barley, diced beef* and water into a pan, bring to the boil, skim, and simmer gently for 1 hour.
3 Add all the prepared vegetables except the cabbage, plenty of seasoning and cook for a further $1\frac{1}{2}$ hours.
4 Add the cabbage and allow another 15 minutes cooking.
5 Skim off any superfluous fat from the broth, pour into hot dish or soup cups and garnish with the parsley.

*If desired the meat can be left in one piece and removed from the soup whole so that it can be used for a separate dish

Sour-hot soup

cooking time   15 minutes

you will need for 4 servings:

4 oz. lean pork	1 tablespoon soya sauce
$\frac{1}{2}$ square ($1\frac{1}{2}$ oz.)	$\frac{1}{2}$ teaspoon pepper
beancurd*	1 tablespoon vinegar
3 dried mushrooms,	2 teaspoons cornflour
soaked*	1 tablespoon water
1 pint stock	1 teaspoon salt
1 tablespoon sherry	$\frac{1}{3}$ teaspoon taste powder†

*Optional—obtainable from shops selling Chinese food
†Sold in good grocers' shops—monosodium glutamate

1 Sliver pork, beancurd and mushrooms.
2 Bring stock to boil and add all three.
3 Simmer 5 minutes.
4 Add sherry, soya sauce, pepper, vinegar and cornflour blended with the water.
5 Cook until soup thickens.
6 Pour over seasoning and stir well.

Poultry and Game Soups

There is no greater waste of money than to discard any poultry or game carcase without using it as a basis for a soup.

The stock may not have enough flavour to make a soup by itself but it does give soup a first-class basis. If, however, there are pieces of flesh still left on the carcase you may find that you have sufficient 'body' without adding a lot of vegetables to detract from the flavour. Recipes on the following page are based on stock.

Cream of chicken soup

cooking time $3\frac{1}{4}$ hours

you will need for 12 servings:

1 small boiling fowl	2 oz. butter
water to cover	2 oz. flour or 1 oz.
bouquet garni (see	cornflour
page 6)	1 pint milk
seasoning	$\frac{1}{4}$ pint cream or
optional vegetables	evaporated milk
(1 carrot, 1 onion,	2 egg yolks
piece celery)	

1 Cut up the fowl if wished or use whole. Cover with cold water, add *bouquet garni,* seasoning and a few vegetables if wished (but too many will kill the delicate flavour of the chicken).
2 Simmer for 2–3 hours until tender.
3 Take all the meat from the bones and rub it through a sieve.
4 Add to the stock to give a smooth thick mixture.
5 Make a sauce of the butter, flour and milk.
6 When thick and creamy add to the chicken mixture and reheat gently.
7 Beat the egg yolks with the cream and add to the soup, then cook gently until thickened again; this takes about 3 minutes. DO NOT BOIL.

Hare soup

cooking time $1\frac{3}{4}$ hours

you will need for 6–8 servings:

bones of a hare	liver, not used in
2 pints water or stock	main dish (blood can
2 onions	also be added to give
2 bay leaves	richness of flavour)
2 small carrots	$\frac{1}{8}$ pint port wine or
piece of turnip	Madeira (optional)
bouquet garni (see	seasoning
page 6)	pinch sugar
head and any other parts	2 oz. dripping, margarine
of hare flesh, such as	or butter

1 Put the bones, meat, diced vegetables, herbs and blood into pan with the water or stock.
2 Bring to the boil and continue cooking gently for $1\frac{1}{2}$ hours.
3 Strain carefully; if any meat is left on the bones this should be sieved, minced or pounded until very fine and returned to the soup.
4 Blend the flour with a little water and add to the soup together with the margarine, butter or dripping.*
5 Bring slowly to the boil and cook until thickened, season then simmer for about 10 minutes.
6 Stir in the wine.

*The fat can be omitted if wished

Variations:

Rabbit soup

Substitute rabbit for hare in previous recipe.

Creamed rabbit or hare soup

Use $1\frac{1}{2}$ pints stock, then make a white sauce with the flour, butter and $\frac{1}{2}$ pint milk. Blend the stock into this.

Chicken soup (with carcase only)

cooking time $1\frac{1}{2}$–2 hours

you will need:

one chicken carcase with	*bouquet garni* (see
a little flesh left on	page 6)
wings etc.	seasoning
water to cover	

1 Put the ingredients into a saucepan and simmer gently for approximately 2 hours.
2 Lift out the carcase and carefully cut any little pieces of meat away from the bones. Do not use the skin.
3 Reheat with the stock and serve.

Chicken soup and dumplings

cooking time $1\frac{1}{2}$–2 hours

you will need for 4 servings:

1 chicken carcase	**For dumplings:**
seasoning	2 oz. flour (with plain
water to cover	flour $\frac{1}{2}$ teaspoon
bouquet garni (see	baking powder)
page 6)	1 oz. margarine, butter
	or shredded suet
	water to bind

1 Simmer the ingredients for approximately $1\frac{1}{2}$ hours.
2 Lift out from the stock, returning any pieces of meat to the pan with seasoning.
3 To prepare dumplings, sieve flour and seasoning then rub in butter or margarine or suet.
4 Mix to a fairly firm consistency with the water —you should be able to roll them in balls with slightly floured hands. (If the dough is too stiff the dumplings will be heavy and solid; if too soft, they will break.)
5 Make sure the liquid is boiling then add the dumplings. Cook steadily for 10–15 minutes.

Variation:

Herb dumplings

Add pinch of mixed herbs or 1–2 teaspoons fresh finely chopped herbs.

Turkey soup

Any of the suggestions for chicken soups could be used with a turkey carcase.

Using duck or goose in soups

It must be remembered that both duck and goose are very fatty and therefore it is better to make a stock, let it cool, lift off the excess fat which will have solidified and then proceed as for other meat or chicken soups. The flavour of the stock is excellent.

Game soups

The carcase of game, unless it has been hung for a very long time and is very 'high', produces a very good stock. For Hare soup it can be flavoured with various vegetables, or it can be used as the basis for a game soup prepared like chicken soup.

Curried poultry or game soups

By adding a little curry powder to the ingredients in either chicken or game stock you do give a very pleasant flavour to this type of soup.

Clear Soups

A clear soup is perhaps the most difficult to make because it must be clarified with the greatest of care. You will find the right way to make clear soup given in the recipe for Beef consommé (this page step 4). By putting in the egg shell and stiffly beaten egg white you collect any minute particles of vegetable, meat and fat which would spoil the clarity of the soup. For family use, of course, the flavour is just as good whether the soup has been cleared or not.

Beef tea

cooking time 2 hours

you will need for 4 servings:

1 lb. lean beef   good pinch salt
1 pint water

1 After removing all fat, cut the meat into small pieces.
2 Put these into a stone jar or double saucepan, adding the water and salt; stand in a saucepan of water.
3 Bring the water in the saucepan just to the boil; then let it simmer very gently for a good 2 hours.
4 Strain the beef tea through muslin, then allow it to cool sufficiently to skim off the fat.
5 Reheat, without boiling, and serve with crisp toast.

Note:

Do not make large quantities of beef tea for it should not be kept for longer than a day.

Beef consommé

cooking time 1 hour

you will need for 4 servings:

12 oz. shin of beef	sprig parsley
2 pints good stock	bay leaf
seasoning	
1 onion	**To clear soup:**
1 carrot	1 dessertspoon sherry,
small piece celery	optional
	1 egg white and shell

1 Cut the meat into small pieces and put these into a saucepan together with the other ingredients.
2 Simmer very gently for 1 hour, then strain through several thicknesses of muslin.
3 Add sherry if desired.
4 To clear consommé put in a stiffly beaten egg white and clean egg shell, gently simmer for a further 20 minutes, then re-strain.

Variations:

Consommé julienne
Add to the above quantity

1 good-sized carrot	small piece cabbage
$\frac{1}{2}$ medium-sized turnip	1 oz. margarine
1 leek or onion	

Cut the vegetables into thin pieces about the size and thickness of a matchstick. Melt margarine in a saucepan and toss the vegetables in this until just turning brown. Add about $\frac{1}{8}$ pint of the consommé and cook gently until the vegetables are quite tender. Take off any fat and add the remaining consommé, reheating gently.

Consommé Celestine
Make thin pancakes (see page 80) then cut into wafer-thin strips. Heat in the consommé.

Consommé au vermicelli
To the quantity of Beef consommé on page 15 add 2 tablespoons vermicelli. Cook gently for 7 minutes, then serve.

Veal consommé
Use same ingredients as Beef consommé plus 12 oz. stewing veal. Leave out the bay leaf and add a very light sherry to keep the pale colour.

Chicken consommé
Allow the stock in which chicken has been simmered to cool, remove the fat and reboil the stock with pieces of vegetable for about 30 minutes. Strain as Beef consommé.

Game consommé
Make a good stock by boiling the carcase of any game together with vegetables. Allow to cool, remove any fat, reheat, strain and flavour with sherry.

Clear chicken or turkey soup

cooking time   2 hours

you will need for 4 servings:

1 chicken or turkey carcase	chopped parsley
2–3 peppercorns	1 carrot
salt and pepper	1 onion
	2 cloves

1 Remove any remaining small pieces of meat from the bones to keep on one side, then break up bones and put in a pan with cut-up vegetables, spices and seasoning.
2 Cover with water and simmer gently for about 2 hours.
3 Strain, add pieces of meat chopped small and chopped parsley; reheat.

Note:

If using a pressure cooker allow 25 minutes at 15 lb. pressure.

Clear mushroom soup
cooking time   10–15 minutes
you will need for 4 servings:

1 small onion (optional)	1¼ pints white stock or water with 1 chicken stock cube
6–8 oz. mushrooms	seasoning

1 Chop the onion very finely and slice the mushrooms.
2 Put into the stock, season and simmer for approximately 10–15 minutes.

Clear tomato soup
cooking time   25 minutes
you will need for 4 servings:

1½ lb. tomatoes	1 small onion, chopped
1 pint water or white stock	1 heaped teaspoon yeast extract
½ small beetroot, preferably uncooked	seasoning
small piece celery	2 bay leaves

1 Put all the ingredients in a large saucepan and cook gently until the tomatoes are very soft. This should take about 25 minutes.
2 Remove the beetroot and bay leaves; rub first through a sieve and then strain through muslin.
3 Reheat or serve cold.
4 If a slightly thickened soup is desired it will only be necessary to rub through the sieve, without straining afterwards.

Mock turtle soup
cooking time   3 hours
you will need for 8–10 servings:

small calf's head	bouquet garni (see page 6)
water	
sherry or Madeira	1 egg white and shell
seasoning	

1 Wash calf's head, split down the centre, remove brains if wished to use for a separate dish (also the tongue can be taken out).
2 Cover with cold water, bring to the boil, throw away the water and cover with fresh water. Add seasoning and herbs and simmer gently until tender—this takes 2–3 hours.
3 Strain off the stock and put into a pan.
4 Cut the meat from the head.
5 Clear the stock as described in Beef consommé (see page 15), add the meat diced; heat gently then put in sherry or Madeira just before serving.

Vegetable Soups

These are possibly the most popular of all soups in that they use reasonably economical ingredients and they can be varied according to vegetables in season. Try not to overcook vegetable soups as both colour and flavour tend to be lost. Although a good stock is often needed, this should not be too strongly flavoured or it will detract from the fresh flavour of the vegetables.

Borshch

cooking time   40 minutes–1½ hours

you will need for 4 servings:

1 large raw beetroot or slightly more cooked beetroot	clove garlic
	2 pints water or stock*
1 carrot	seasoning
1 onion	vinegar
2–3 tomatoes	little sour cream or cream cheese
little chopped celery	

*Use only 1½ pints with cooked beetroot

1 Grate the beetroot and put into pan with the grated or chopped carrot and onion, tomatoes, crushed garlic and celery.
2 Add the stock.
3 Simmer raw beetroot for 1½ hours or cooked beetroot for about 40 minutes.
4 Season and add a little vinegar.
5 Top with sour cream or cream cheese before serving.

Variations:

Jellied borshch

Dissolve about 1 level tablespoon powdered gelatine in the soup after cooking. Allow to cool, but not set, then stir in sour cream. Serve in soup cups and top with cream cheese.

Cranberry borshch

Follow the Borshch recipe above but use 6 oz. cranberries instead of beetroot and omit carrot and onion. You may need a little sugar to take away the 'bite' from the cranberry borshch. Cook for 25 minutes only.

Cream of artichoke soup

cooking time   45 minutes

you will need for 4 servings:

1½ lb. artichokes	½ oz. flour
1 pint water or white stock	¼–½ pint milk
¼ teaspoon vinegar	
seasoning	**To garnish:**
2 oz. butter	paprika

1 Wash and peel the artichokes and, if large, cut into small pieces.
2 Remember to keep the artichokes in cold water, with a tablespoon of lemon juice to preserve a good colour, until ready to cook them.
3 Put into a saucepan with the water or stock, vinegar and seasoning.
4 Simmer gently for a good 30 minutes.
5 Rub through a sieve, then return the purée to the saucepan together with the butter.
6 Blend flour with the cold milk, stir into boiling purée and continue cooking, stirring all the time until it forms a smooth thick sauce.
7 Garnish with paprika and serve with toast.
8 A few of the artichokes can be saved and cut into tiny pieces to put into the soup as a garnish.

Variations:

Cream of beetroot soup

Use raw beetroot. Dice and simmer for approximately 1 hour. Continue as above.

Cream of carrot soup

Ingredients as Cream of artichoke soup, but add a pinch of sugar when cooking the carrots. Omit lemon juice and vinegar.

Cream of potato soup

Follow recipe for artichoke soup but add a little cream, if possible, just before serving.

Cream of turnip soup

All turnips, unless very young, tend to be rather strong in a soup so use ¾ lb. turnips and ¾ lb. potatoes and follow recipe for Cream of artichoke soup.

Cabbage soup

cooking time   1¼ hours

you will need for 4 servings:

2 oz. haricot beans
1 very small cabbage
2 leeks
small carrot
piece turnip
stick celery
1 potato
1 small onion
3 oz. butter
3 pints water

bouquet garni (see page 6)
seasoning
2–4 oz. fat bacon or pork

To garnish:
bread croûtons (see page 8)

1 Soak haricot beans for several hours in cold water.
2 Drain.
3 Dice vegetables and toss in the hot butter for about 10 minutes.
4 Add water and rest of ingredients.
5 Simmer for 1 hour.
6 Rub through a sieve and reheat.*
7 Garnish with bread croûtons.

*The pieces of pork can be removed before sieving and served separately

Cauliflower soup

cooking time   30–35 minutes

you will need:

1 medium cauliflower
1 onion
1 pint water or white stock
seasoning

1 oz. butter
1 oz. flour
½ pint milk

To garnish:
cayenne pepper

1 Cut up cauliflower stalk and some of the flowers, reserving the rest.
2 Put into a pan with the chopped onion, water and seasoning and simmer gently until tender.
3 Rub through a sieve.
4 Make white sauce from the butter, flour and milk; put in the cauliflower purée and reheat, adding a little extra milk if too thick.
5 Meanwhile divide the rest of the flowerets into very small pieces. Boil in salted water until just tender.
6 Put into the soup and garnish with cayenne pepper.

Variations:

Cream of cauliflower soup
Use a little less water and add cream after blending cauliflower purée with the sauce.

Cheese and cauliflower soup
Add 2–3 oz. grated cheese to the soup and heat until melted.

Golden ball cauliflower soup
Blend the yolk of 1 egg with a little cream. Stir into the soup just before serving and thicken without boiling. Garnish with hard-boiled egg yolk, rubbed through a sieve to look like mimosa balls.

Cream of celery soup

cooking time   30 minutes

you will need for 4 servings:

1 good-sized head celery
1½ pints stock or water
1 oz. flour
2 oz. butter
¼ pint milk
¼ pint cream or evaporated milk

seasoning, including celery salt

To garnish:
cayenne pepper

1 If you do not wish to sieve this soup, cut the celery into very tiny pieces.
2 Simmer celery with the water or stock until tender, then sieve if wished.
3 Meanwhile make a white sauce from the flour, butter and milk: this will be very thick, so the celery mixture or purée needs to be blended very slowly into this. Reheat, then add the cream and seasoning.
4 Garnish with cayenne pepper.

Chestnut soup

cooking time   1 hour 10 minutes

you will need for 4 servings:

1 lb. chestnuts
1 pint water or white stock
2 oz. margarine or butter

½ pint milk
good pinch salt, cayenne pepper, and sugar if liked

1 Split the skins of the chestnuts, cover with water and cook for 15 minutes.
2 Peel the nuts while still hot, then return to the saucepan with the water or stock.
3 Simmer gently for 45 minutes.
4 Rub the chestnuts through a sieve and put the purée into the pan, together with the butter or margarine, milk and seasoning.

5 Heat slowly, then serve with crisp pieces of toast or croûtons of bread.

Cucumber purée soup

cooking time   20 minutes

you will need for 4 servings:

1 large or 2 medium cucumbers*	1 oz. flour
	½ pint milk
1 onion	seasoning
little celery	
¾ pint white stock	**To garnish:**
1 oz. butter	parsley

*If all the skin is left on a cucumber it gives a very bitter flavour but a little should be included to give a slight green colour. Alternatively, the cucumber can be simmered in water for a few minutes before using for this recipe

1 Chop the cucumber and onion and mix with the chopped celery.
2 If celery is not obtainable chicory or celeriac can be used instead.
3 Put into a pan with the stock and simmer until tender.
4 Rub through a sieve.
5 Meanwhile make a white sauce with the butter, flour and milk, add the cucumber purée and reheat.
6 Season well.
7 A little lemon juice or vinegar can be added when heated but do not boil again.
8 Garnish with chopped parsley.

Lentil soup

cooking time   1½ hours

you will need for 4 servings:

8 oz. washed lentils	1 oz. butter
4 oz. bacon, chopped	½ oz. flour
1 onion, chopped	½ pint milk
1 carrot	
1 pint water or stock	
seasoning	**To garnish:**
little chopped thyme or parsley	chopped parsley

1 Put the lentils (these can be soaked overnight if wished), bacon, onion, carrots and stock into a casserole and add seasoning and herbs—the seasoning MUST be added at the very start of cooking.
2 Cover and simmer gently for about 1½ hours.
3 Meanwhile make a very thin sauce with the butter, flour and milk, add the lentil purée and reheat.
4 Check seasoning and serve garnished with chopped parsley.

Variations:

Lentil and celery soup
Use about 6 oz. lentils and 4 oz. chopped celery.

Lentil and tomato soup
Use 4 oz. lentils only and 8 oz. tomatoes.

Cream of mushroom soup

cooking time   15–20 minutes

you will need for 4 servings:

8 oz. mushrooms*	1 pint water or stock
2 oz. butter or margarine	¾ pint milk
	seasoning
2 oz. flour	

*Mushroom stalks can be used

1 Chop mushrooms finely unless you wish to strain the soup.
2 Melt margarine or butter in saucepan, fry mushrooms for 5 minutes, stirring to prevent their discolouring.
3 Stir in the flour and cook for 3 minutes.
4 Remove the pan from the heat and gradually add water and milk.
5 Bring to the boil and cook until soup thickens.
6 Season.

Cream of onion soup

cooking time   30 minutes

you will need for 4 servings:

8 oz. onions	2 pints milk
1 oz. butter	2 egg yolks
2 tablespoons cornflour	3 tablespoons cream
	seasoning

1 Chop and gently fry the onions in the hot butter until tender, but do not brown.
2 Add the cornflour and mix in well, then cook for a further minute.
3 Add the milk and cook gently for about 20 minutes.
4 Mix egg yolks and cream together, add a little soup, then return all to the saucepan and reheat without boiling.
5 Season to taste.

Crème Olga

cooking time   35–40 minutes

you will need for 4 servings:

8 oz. spring onions	seasoning
2 oz. mushrooms	1 egg yolk
2 medium potatoes	4 tablespoons cream
1 oz. butter	
1½ pints milk	**To garnish:**
bayleaf	croûtons (see page 8)

1 Slice onions, mushrooms and potatoes and cook slowly in the butter until soft but not coloured.
2 Add the milk, bayleaf and seasoning.
3 Simmer 20 minutes.
4 Rub through a fine sieve, return to the pan and stir until boiling.
5 Simmer a few minutes then remove from heat.
6 Add egg yolk blended with cream and reheat carefully.
7 Adjust the seasoning and serve with croûtons.

Low-calorie spinach soup

cooking time   30 minutes

you will need for 4 servings:

1 lb. fresh spinach or small packet frozen spinach	½ pint water
	½ pint milk (without cream)
1 small onion	a little grated nutmeg
seasoning	

1 Cook the spinach with onion, seasoning and water until tender.
2 Rub through a sieve, add to the milk with grated nutmeg and reheat.
3 Serve to those people who are watching their weight first, and stir in a knob of butter and one or two tablespoons of top of the milk or cream for the rest of the family.
4 This is a fairly filling soup and therefore small quantities are sufficient for most people.

Variation:

You can use ½ pint tomato juice instead of water or cook 1–2 tomatoes with the spinach.

Creamed spinach soup

cooking time   25 minutes

you will need for 4 servings:

1 lb. spinach or 1 small packet frozen spinach	3 tablespoons cream
	nutmeg
1 oz. butter	seasoning
1 small onion, sliced	
1 oz. cornflour	
1½ pints milk	**To garnish:**
2 egg yolks	croûtons (see page 8)

1 Cook and sieve the spinach.
2 Heat the butter in a saucepan and sauté the onion until tender but not brown.
3 Add the cornflour, mix well and cook for a few minutes.
4 Add the milk, stir until boiling and boil for 3 minutes.
5 Strain the sauce on to the spinach, then return to the heat.
6 Mix the egg yolks and cream, add a little of the soup, then return all to the saucepan.
7 Add seasonings and reheat gently for several minutes before serving. DO NOT ALLOW TO BOIL.
8 Garnish with croûtons.

Minestrone soup

cooking time   2 hours 10 minutes

you will need for 4 servings:

3 oz. haricot beans	8 oz. tomatoes (bottled or fresh)
1 large onion	
2 tablespoons olive oil	8 oz. finely shredded cabbage
1 clove garlic	
1–2 oz. diced bacon	2 oz. macaroni
seasoning	
1½ pints water or stock	**To garnish:**
1 large diced carrot	1 tablespoon chopped parsley
2 tablespoons chopped celery	grated Parmesan cheese

1 Soak the haricot beans overnight in water.
2 Chop onion finely and toss in the hot oil, together with the crushed garlic and bacon.
3 Add haricot beans, seasoning and water and simmer gently for about 1½ hours.
4 Put in rest of vegetables, with the exception of the cabbage, and cook for a further 20 minutes, adding a little more water if necessary.
5 Add cabbage and macaroni and cook until both are just tender.
6 Taste and add seasoning if necessary.
7 Serve with chopped parsley and top with the cheese.

Note:

A little red wine can be used in this recipe; put this in with the vegetables.

French onion soup

cooking time   40 minutes

you will need for 4 servings:

1–1½ lb. onions	2 oz. grated cheese (preferably Gruyère)
1–2 oz. butter or good beef dripping	4 slices toast or French bread
2 pints brown stock	
seasoning	

1 Melt the fat in a saucepan.
2 Slice the onions thinly and fry in the hot fat until a pale golden brown.
3 Add the liquid and seasoning.
4 Bring slowly to the boil, lower the heat and simmer gently for ½ hour.
5 Put each slice of hot toast on a soup plate; pour over the soup and sprinkle with cheese.

Variation:

French onion soup gratinée

Use ingredients for above recipe but put cheese-topped soup under grill for 2–3 minutes until cheese melts.

Pea soup

cooking time   35–40 minutes

you will need for 4 servings:

1½ lb. peas (including pods) or pods from 2 lb. fresh peas when young	good pinch sugar
	good knob butter
1½ pints water or ham stock	
small onion (if desired)	**To garnish:**
seasoning	chopped mint or fried bread croûtons (see page 8) or peas, if required
small sprig mint	

1 Wash pods and shell.
2 Put pods and peas into a saucepan with stock (reserving few peas if required for garnish), onion, seasoning and mint, and simmer until tender.
3 Rub through a sieve; this must be done very vigorously, so that the flesh of the pods is pushed through and only the skins are left.
4 Return to the pan, reheat, adding a little sugar to taste and a good knob of butter. If the pods are very fleshy the soup may be a little thick when sieved so add a small quantity of extra stock or milk.
5 Serve garnished with a few freshly cooked peas or chopped mint or croûtons.

Spring soup

cooking time   40 minutes

you will need for 4 servings:

12 small spring onions	1 pint white stock or water
½ small lettuce	
2 oz. margarine or butter	2 teaspoons flour
few small carrots	3 tablespoons milk
	seasoning
	1 egg

1 Slice the onions and shred the lettuce.
2 Heat 1 oz. of the margarine or butter in a saucepan and toss in half the onion and all the lettuce and carrots.
3 Add the stock and simmer gently for 30 minutes.
4 Rub through a sieve, then return to the pan.
5 Blend the flour with the milk and add this together with seasoning.
6 Bring slowly to the boil and cook until slightly thickened (the amount of thickening is very small in this recipe).
7 Heat the remaining 1 oz. margarine or butter and fry the rest of the onions.
8 Take the soup off the heat for a few minutes and stir in the well-beaten egg—do not cook again.
9 Serve garnished with the fried onions.

Cream of tomato soup

cooking time   1¼ hours

you will need for 4 servings:

1 lb. tomatoes	*bouquet garni*
1 onion	¾ oz. cornflour
1 carrot	¼–½ pint milk
1 stick celery	pinch sugar
little fat bacon	
1½ pints stock	**To garnish:**
salt	chopped white of egg or croûtons (see page 8)
pepper	

1 Slice the vegetables.
2 Fry the bacon slowly to extract the fat, then add the vegetables and fry for about 10 minutes.
3 Add the stock (or water), seasoning and *bouquet garni*, bring to the boil and simmer gently until tender—about 1 hour.
4 Remove the *bouquet garni* and bacon, rub the soup through a fine sieve, and add the cornflour blended with the milk.
5 Return to the pan, bring just to the boil, stirring well, and cook gently for 2–3 minutes.
6 Check seasoning, add the sugar and serve with your chosen garnish.

Variation:

Tomato soup

Ingredients as Cream of tomato soup but omit cornflour and milk. Cook the tomatoes and vegetables. Rub through a sieve, return to the pan and garnish with parsley or fried bread croûtons (see page 8).

Tomato and rice broth

cooking time   25–30 minutes

you will need for 4 servings:

1½ pints tomato juice or 8 oz. tomatoes and 1 pint water	1 diced carrot salt pepper
2 oz. rice	
1 diced onion	
little diced celery or celeriac	**To garnish:** grated Cheddar cheese

1 If using tomatoes they should be simmered in the water or stock, then the liquid strained off, the tomatoes sieved and added to liquid.
2 Add the rice to boiling tomato liquid together with the diced vegetables.
3 Season well and cook for about 20 minutes until rice and vegetables are tender.
4 Serve with the grated cheese.

Tomato and vegetable soup

cooking time   10 minutes

you will need for 4 servings:

1 small packet mixed frozen vegetables (or tin mixed vegetables or 1 grated potato, 2 grated carrots, 1 grated onion, few peas)	1 bottle or tin tomato juice
	½ pint water (or liquid from tinned vegetables)
seasoning	**To garnish:** little grated cheese

1 Put all ingredients, except cheese, into pan and simmer until tender.
2 Serve topped with cheese.

Cream of vegetable soup

cooking time   45 minutes

you will need for 4 servings:

1¼–1½ lb. mixed vegetables*	2 oz. butter
1 pint water or white stock	½ oz. flour
¼ teaspoon vinegar	¼–½ pint milk
seasoning	**To garnish:** paprika and/or parsley

*Choose a good selection: because only a small amount of flour is used include 1 or 2 vegetables like potatoes and carrots which give thickening. Tomatoes and/or carrots will give colour. A small quantity of green vegetables can be added but avoid too many very strongly flavoured vegetables such as turnips—a mixed vegetable soup should have a good balance of flavours

1 Wash and peel the vegetables and, if large, cut into small pieces. Keep them in cold water as you prepare them until they are ready to cook: if you have included any artichokes add 1 tablespoon lemon juice to keep colour.

2 Put into a saucepan with water or stock, vinegar and seasoning.
3 Simmer gently for a good 30 minutes.
4 Rub through a sieve, then return purée to saucepan, adding the butter.
5 Blend the flour with the cold milk, stir into the boiling purée and continue cooking, stirring all the time, until it forms a smooth thick soup.
6 Garnish with paprika and/or parsley.

Vichyssoise

cooking time   40 minutes

you will need for 4 servings:

2 oz. butter	1 tablespoon parsley, chopped
2 large onions, chopped	
8 medium leeks, chopped	2 eggs or egg yolks
1½ pints chicken stock or water with 2 chicken stock cubes	¼ pint cream or milk seasoning
2 medium potatoes, chopped	**To garnish:** chopped chives or parsley

1 Heat the butter and fry chopped onions and leeks until golden but not brown.
2 Add stock, or water with chicken stock cubes, chopped potatoes and parsley.
3 Simmer for 30 minutes, rub through a sieve and return to the pan.
4 Blend the eggs with the cream, add to soup and cook WITHOUT BOILING for a few minutes.
5 Season.
6 Serve topped with chives or parsley.

Watercress soup

cooking time   11 minutes

you will need for 4 servings:

2 bunches watercress (about 4 oz.)	1 pint water
1 tablespoon corn oil	½ oz. cornflour
2 good teaspoons yeast extract	5 tablespoons milk

1 Wash the watercress thoroughly, reserve few sprigs for garnish, and remove leaves from stalks of remainder.
2 Sauté gently for 2–3 minutes in heated oil.
3 Add yeast extract and the water.
4 Bring to the boil, stirring, then simmer for about 5 minutes.
5 Sieve if required.
6 Mix cornflour and milk smoothly, add to the purée and cook for 3 minutes, stirring all the time.
7 Garnish with sprigs of watercress.

Soups that Make a Meal

To save preparing an elaborate meal, make a really satisfying and sustaining soup that can be a meal in itself. The British broths, American chowders and Continental bisques are all satisfying soups that are almost too filling for the first course of a meal. Served with cheese and fruit they are the answer to a one-course meal.

Vegetable soups

Celery chowder

cooking time   30–35 minutes

you will need for 4 servings:

8–10 oz. celery	½ oz. flour
1 onion	½ pint milk
2 medium potatoes	
½ pint white stock or	**To garnish:**
water	celery tips or croûtons
seasoning	(see page 8)
1 oz. butter	

1 Chop the celery into very tiny pieces, chop or grate the onion and cut the potatoes into small dice.
2 Simmer together in the stock or water until tender, seasoning well.
3 Meanwhile make a thin sauce of the butter, flour and milk, add vegetable mixture to this.
4 Heat thoroughly, check seasoning and serve garnished with tiny celery tips or croûtons.

Vegetable chowder

cooking time   23 minutes

you will need for 4 servings:

1 can or packet	**To garnish:**
vegetable soup	little chopped parsley
2 potatoes	little grated cheese

1 Make up soup as directed on packet or heat contents of tin.
2 When the mixture begins to boil add the diced potatoes and cook for 20 minutes.
3 Top with chopped parsley and grated cheese before serving.

Fish soups

Fish soups are really at their best if not sieved, but served like a chowder (which is almost a stew). They are then a perfect dish for a main meal. You will get a better flavour if you simmer the bones and skin of white fish, or the shell of lobster, crab, prawns, etc. to give you stock.

Lobster chowder

cooking time   25–30 minutes

you will need for 4 servings:

1 small lobster	1 medium potato, diced
1 pint water	⅜ pint milk or cream
1–2 rashers bacon	good pinch sugar
1 teaspoon finely	salt
chopped onion	pepper
1½ oz. flour	crisp toast fingers

1 Remove flesh from lobster, cut in small pieces and put aside.
2 Put shell only into pan with the water and simmer gently for about 15 minutes.
3 Strain and add enough water to make up to 1 pint again.
4 After removing rind, cut bacon into narrow strips.
5 Put into a pan and fry lightly; add the onion and flour and cook gently without colouring.
6 Gradually add the lobster stock, stirring all the time.
7 When the sauce has come to the boil and thickened, add lobster, cut into small pieces, and the rest of the ingredients.
8 Either reduce heat under pan to cook very gently or put in double saucepan and cook until it forms a thick creamy mixture.
9 Serve with crisp fingers of toast.

New England clam chowder

cooking time   30 minutes

you will need for 4 servings:

8 oz. salt pork, chopped	$\frac{1}{8}$ teaspoon pepper
3 small onions	2 cans clams
1$\frac{1}{2}$ pints boiling water	1$\frac{1}{2}$ pints milk
12 oz. potatoes, diced	6 water biscuits

1 Chop the pork and fry in a large saucepan.
2 Add the onions and sauté until browned.
3 Add boiling water, potatoes and pepper and boil about 15 minutes, or until potatoes are soft.
4 Mince and heat clams and any liquor; add with milk to mixture and bring to the boil.
5 Pour chowder over crumbled water biscuits in soup dishes.

Variation:

Oyster chowder

Approximately 16–20 oysters could be used in place of clams.

Salmon chowder

cooking time   20 minutes

you will need for 4 servings:

1 packet tomato or tomato and vegetable, or vegetable soup	1 clove garlic, crushed (optional)
1$\frac{1}{2}$ pints water	1 green pepper, finely chopped
2 oz. tiny shell pasta or noodles	1 medium can salmon

1 Make up the soup with 1$\frac{1}{2}$ pints of water (or as directed on the packet) and bring to boil.
2 Add the pasta and crushed garlic and simmer gently until pasta is tender.
3 Add the finely chopped green pepper and flaked salmon then heat together.

. . . but watch the waistline

Low-calorie fish chowder

cooking time   25–30 minutes

you will need for 4 servings:

8 oz. white fish	good pinch sugar
1–2 rashers bacon	salt
1 onion, finely chopped	pepper
1 pint fish stock or water	
1 medium potato, diced	**To garnish:**
$\frac{1}{4}$ pint milk	parsley
	paprika

1 Cut the fish into neat cubes, using any skin and bones for stock as described on page 7.
2 Remove the rind from the bacon and cut into small pieces.
3 Fry with the chopped onion without allowing it to colour.
4 Add the fish stock, the pieces of fish, potato, milk and seasoning, and sugar.
5 Simmer gently for about 15 minutes, then serve topped with parsley and paprika.

Variations:

To make a richer chowder, add an egg blended with a little of the milk for the last 5 minutes and cook WITHOUT BOILING until thickened. A little corn-on-the-cob (which is fairly high in calories) makes a most attractive addition to this soup. Diced cucumber, which is low in calories, can be added to give extra texture as well as flavour.

Slimmer's chowder

cooking time   35 minutes

you will need for 4 servings:

1 oz. margarine	2 medium carrots
1 large onion	seasoning
1–2 small rashers bacon	2 pints water with little yeast extract to flavour
2 large tomatoes	
2 sticks celery	$\frac{1}{4}$ small cabbage
$\frac{1}{2}$ large or 1 small green pepper	
very few mushrooms (optional)	**To garnish:** chopped parsley

1 Melt the margarine and fry diced onion until just changing colour, then put in the chopped bacon and continue to cook for a few minutes.
2 Skin and chop tomatoes and add with all the other diced vegetables (except the cabbage) and the water mixed with the yeast extract cube—the tomatoes will become part of the liquid with cooking.
3 Cook steadily for approximately 20 minutes.
4 Add the finely chopped cabbage and cook for a further 10 minutes.
5 Garnish with chopped parsley.

Note:

To make a more satisfying dish for non-slimming members of the family, add a thick layer of grated cheese on top before serving.

Soups to Serve Cold

All too often soup is considered only as a hot dish, but in hot weather, or if you have a hot main course, a really delicious cold soup is an excellent start to the meal. Make sure your cold soups have a slight bite about them for their purpose is to sharpen one's appetite.

Jellied and thin soups

Jellied consommé

cooking time   1 hour

you will need for 4 servings:

12 oz. shin of beef	sprig parsley
2 pints strong stock	bayleaf
seasoning	
1 onion	**To garnish:**
1 carrot	cucumber or lemon or
small piece celery	smoked salmon

1 Make consommé using method on page 15 and allow to cool, when it will set into a light jelly.
2 If the weather is hot and you have no refrigerator, dissolve 2 level teaspoons powdered gelatine in consommé to help it to set.
3 Beat lightly before putting in soup cups.
4 Garnish with slices of cucumber or lemon or smoked salmon.

Jellied two-tone consommé

cooking time   1 hour

you will need for 4 servings:

1 pint beef consommé (see page 15)	2 level teaspoons powdered gelatine
1 pint chicken consommé (see page 16)	little sherry

1 Put the consommés to heat in two separate pans.
2 Soften the gelatine in a small amount of sherry and add half to the beef and half to the chicken consommé.

3 Allow to dissolve.
4 Let the two kinds of soup set lightly.
5 Whisk, and put a layer of light and a layer of dark consommé in separate cups or cut into cubes and arrange in the soup cups.
6 Serve very cold.

Consommé Florida

cooking time $1\frac{1}{2}$ hours

you will need for 4 servings:

$1\frac{1}{2}$ pints consommé (see page 15)	1–2 oranges
	1 small green pepper
2 large firm tomatoes	

1 Peel oranges and add most of flesh to the consommé together with most of the chopped flesh of the green pepper and the skinned and seeded tomato pulp, reserving some of each for garnish.
2 Simmer gently for 30 minutes, then strain.
3 Serve very cold, garnished with tiny pieces of orange, raw tomato and tiny strips of green pepper.

Iced cucumber soup

cooking time   15 minutes

you will need for 4 servings:

1 medium cucumber	$\frac{1}{8}$ pint milk or evaporated
1 small onion, chopped	milk
$\frac{1}{2}$ oz. butter	
$\frac{1}{2}$ pint stock	**To garnish:**
seasoning	lemon

1 Cut cucumber into pieces, leaving on some of the peel.
2 Fry onion in butter, add cucumber, half the stock, seasoning and simmer gently for about 15 minutes.
3 Put through sieve.
4 Add milk and rest of stock to purée; when cold pour into freezing tray and leave until lightly frosted.
5 Serve in soup cups garnished with lemon.

Jellied gazpacho

cooking time   5—8 minutes

you will need for 4 servings:

1 beef or chicken bouillon cube	½ cucumber, peeled, seeded and chopped
¾ pint boiling water	1 small onion, chopped
1 15-oz. can tomato juice (¾ pint)	2 tablespoons corn oil
½ oz. gelatine	2 tablespoons vinegar
2 tomatoes, peeled and chopped	**To garnish:**
½ green pepper, seeded and chopped	lemon slices

1 Dissolve the beef or chicken bouillon cube in the boiling water.
2 Put into a pan with tomato juice and gelatine, and heat until the gelatine has dissolved.
3 Leave to cool.
4 Meanwhile steep the vegetables in the corn oil and vinegar.
5 When the liquid is almost set, strain through a very fine sieve or muslin.
6 Pour on to the vegetables and chill until jellied.
7 Break up with a fork, pile into glasses and garnish with lemon slices.
8 Serve with French bread.

Thick soups

Gazpacho

no cooking time

you will need for 4 servings:

water	1 small green pepper
1 lb. tomatoes	seasoning
1 medium cucumber	little olive oil
1 onion or several spring onions	lemon juice or white wine vinegar
1 or 2 cloves garlic	

1 Put the water in the refrigerator to become very cold.
2 Skin the tomatoes as this helps when the mixture is sieved, or blended in an electric blender, to give a smooth mixture.
3 Peel the cucumber and cut into very small dice, saving a little as garnish.
4 Chop the tomatoes, onion and garlic; add to the cucumber and either pound until smooth or rub through a sieve; the pepper can also be sieved or chopped very finely, after removing all the seeds and core. (If using an electric liquidiser you will need to add a little water so none of the thick mixture is wasted.)
5 Put the purée into basin, then gradually beat in

seasoning, olive oil and enough cold water to give a flowing consistency.
6 Taste to check seasoning and add lemon juice or vinegar.
7 Serve garnished with remaining cucumber.
8 This soup must be very cold so put in the refrigerator until ready to serve and serve in ice-cold soup cups.

Chilled mushroom soup

cooking time   15 minutes

you will need for 4 servings:

1 packet mushroom soup powder	green food colouring, optional
1¼ pints water	
¼ pint cream or evaporated milk	**To garnish:**
1 tablespoon white wine	lemon slices

1 Make up the soup powder with 1¼ pints water, cooking as directed.
2 Leave until completely cold, then add the cream or milk, white wine, and food colouring if desired.
3 Garnish with lemon slices.

Summer soup

cooking time   20—25 minutes

you will need for 4 servings:

1—2 medium potatoes	pinch dry mustard
4—5 inches cucumber, chopped but not peeled	¾ pint chicken stock, or water and bouillon cube
2—3 sprigs parsley	1 small onion, sliced
salt	¼ pint milk or thin cream
pepper	

1 Cook all the ingredients except the milk or cream in the chicken stock until potatoes are tender.
2 Force everything through a medium sieve, add the milk or cream and season.
3 This soup is equally good hot or cold, but if it is to be served cold it should be well chilled for at least 2—3 hours.

Iced tomato soup

cooking time   20 minutes

you will need for 4 servings:

1½ lb. tomatoes	1 teaspoon vinegar or lemon juice
1 pint water or white stock	seasoning
½ small beetroot	2 bay leaves
1 small piece of celery	
1 small chopped onion	**To garnish:**
few drops Worcester- shire sauce	lemon slices

1 Put all the ingredients into a pan and cook until the tomatoes are soft.
2 Removing beetroot, rub rest of mixture through a sieve and pour into the freezing tray of the refrigerator.
3 Leave for a short time until iced, then serve in cold cups topped with lemon rings.

Chilled vegetable chowder

cooking time 15 minutes

you will need for 4 servings:

1 packet thick vegetable soup	**To garnish:** chopped chives or parsley
1 pint water	
$\frac{1}{4}$ pint milk	
$\frac{1}{4}$ pint cream or yoghourt	

1 Blend the thick vegetable soup powder with the water.
2 Put into a pan and cook until tender.
3 Allow to cool, then stir in the milk, cream or yoghourt, and put into the refrigerator until very cold.
4 Put into cups and garnish with chives or parsley.

Watercress cream soup

cooking time 20 minutes

you will need for 4–6 servings:

4 oz. watercress	$1\frac{3}{4}$ pints chicken stock or water and 2 chicken bouillon cubes
1 small onion	
1 oz. margarine or butter	little whipped cream
3 medium potatoes	

1 Coarsely chop watercress (reserving few leaves for garnish), chop onion and fry both in the margarine until the onion is pale golden.
2 Add the peeled, sliced potatoes and stock.
3 Bring to the boil, cover and simmer until the potatoes are soft.
4 Rub through a sieve and return to pan.
5 Add the cream, season if necessary, chill and serve in soup cups garnished with leaves of watercress.
6 Dredge lightly with paprika and serve with Melba toast (see page 8).

Note:
This may be served hot on a cold day.

Fruit soups

In hot weather a cold fruit soup is a most delicious beginning to a meal. It should have enough bite to make one feel hungry, so do not oversweeten the fruit. It is customary to serve fruit soups cold but they can be heated if preferred.

Apple soup

cooking time 20 minutes

you will need for 4 servings:

1 lb. fairly sharp cooking apples	sugar to taste
1 pint water	**To garnish:** lemon rings
$\frac{1}{2}$ pint white wine	

1 Chop the apples but do not peel or core.
2 Simmer in the water until tender then rub through a sieve.
3 Add to the white wine.
4 Taste and stir in required sugar while the apple mixture is still sufficiently warm to make it dissolve completely.
5 Serve really cold in soup cups, garnished with lemon rings.

Variations:

Apple and lemon soup
Add the grated rind and juice of 1 lemon to the apples.

Apple and orange soup
Add the grated rind and juice of 2 oranges to the apples.

Spiced apples
Add 1 teaspoon mixed spice to the apples when cooking.

Lemon soup

cooking time 8 minutes

you will need for 4 servings:

1 pint chicken stock or water and 2 chicken stock cubes	2 tablespoons lemon juice
	1 egg
	seasoning

1 Heat the stock.
2 Beat the lemon juice and egg.
3 Whisk into the stock together with seasoning and simmer without boiling for a few minutes.

Iced cherry soup

cooking time   25 minutes

you will need for 4 servings:

1½ lb. or 1 can cherries   **To garnish:**
juice 1 lemon   mint
water
sugar to taste

1 Cover fruit with water.
2 Simmer gently, adding lemon juice and sugar to taste.
3 Reserving few cherries for garnish, rub through sieve and pour into freezing trays to lightly freeze.
4 Serve in soup cups decorated with remaining whole cherries and mint leaves.

Variations:

Cherry plum soup

Use the rather 'sharp' small plums known as cherry plums. A very little white wine added to the mixture gives an excellent flavour.

Crab apple soup

This is made like the Iced cherry soup. Add a little cider if wished and garnish with wedges of lemon.

Cranberry soup

Substituting cranberries, use method for Iced cherry soup—you will need extra sweetening. Mixed soft fruits such as red currants and raspberries can also be used.

Soups that are Different

These soups are not based on vegetable or fish but depend on ingredients one does not normally use as a basis for soup. They are, however, easily made and extremely delicious.

Red wine soup

cooking time   10 minutes

you will need for 4–6 servings:

1 pint inexpensive   4 whole cloves
   red wine   ½ pint water
good pinch ground   3 egg yolks
   cinnamon   little pepper
1 teaspoon sugar

1 Bring the wine, cinnamon, sugar, cloves and water to the boil and simmer without boiling for about 8 minutes.
2 Pour over the beaten egg yolks, stirring well, and add a little pepper to taste.
3 Serve at once, hot.

Note:

This can be chilled if liked, and served with 1 tablespoon yoghourt or sour cream on each plate or soup cup.

Variation:

White wine soup

Use an inexpensive white wine instead of red. This must be dry, not sweet, and it is nicer served cold.

Hollandaise cream soup

cooking time   12–15 minutes

you will need for 4 servings:

1 oz. butter   seasoning
scant 1 oz. cornflour   ½ teaspoon chopped
1½ pints chicken or   tarragon
   veal stock or water   ½ teaspoon chopped
   with 1 chicken   parsley
   bouillon cube
3 egg yolks   **To garnish:**
¼ pint cream   few peas

1 Melt the butter in a pan, add the cornflour and cook for several minutes.
2 Gradually add the stock, bring to boil and boil for 3 minutes, stirring all the time.
3 Beat together the egg yolks and cream and stir carefully into the soup: cook WITHOUT BOILING for a few minutes, stirring all the time.
4 Lastly add the seasoning, tarragon and parsley, and if liked garnish with cold peas.

Variations:

Hollandaise rice soup

Cook 1½ oz. rice in the stock for approximately 10 minutes then proceed as above.

Hollandaise lemon soup

Method as above but add ½ teaspoon very finely grated lemon rind and 2 tablespoons lemon juice at stage 4, taking care that the soup does not boil.

Cheese soup

cooking time   25 minutes

you will need for 4 servings:

1 onion, finely chopped
2 oz. butter
1½ oz. flour
1 pint milk
1 pint stock
2 teaspoons salt
pinch pepper

8 oz. grated Cheddar
   cheese
3 carrots, finely chopped
   or grated
2 sticks celery or piece
   of celeriac, finely
   chopped or grated

1 Sauté the onion in the butter until tender.
2 Add the flour and cook slowly for a minute, stirring well.
3 Add the milk, stock, and seasoning gradually, stirring continually, and bring to the boil.
4 Add the grated cheese and stir until melted.
5 Add carrots and celery, and cook until the vegetables are tender.
6 Serve hot with caraway seed toast fingers (see page 8).

Using Ready-prepared Soups

There is a great variety of soups on the market today, the main groups being:

1 *Canned* soups that need little, if any, diluting.
2 *Concentrated* or, as they are often called, condensed soups which need to be diluted with an equal quantity of liquid—the soup can be varied by using either milk, water, stock or a mixture of stock and milk, or even, in some cases, a little wine. (These soups can also be used as sauces or for gravy.)
3 *Dehydrated soups* which need a considerable amount of liquid which can be varied to give individual flavour—these need cooking for a long time as the ingredients are not pre-cooked.

This chapter gives ideas on mixing prepared soups, the way in which additional ingredients can be put in and suggests how to garnish them to give a 'home-made' look.

Asparagus soup

To serve hot

Heat or cook the canned or packet soup, then try one of the following ideas:

1 Stir in an egg beaten with 2–3 tablespoons cream and heat WITHOUT BOILING. Garnish with paprika.
2 Float tiny balls of soft cream cheese and chopped parsley on the soup just before serving.
3 Top with finely grated Parmesan cheese and a very small amount finely grated lemon rind.

To serve cold

This is delicious before a hot main course, even in winter. Add little lemon juice or white wine and cream to the cold cooked soup. Float wafer-thin lemon rings on top.

Note:

Asparagus is not a good soup to mix with other soups, except chicken or a creamed chicken soup, as its delicate flavour is easily lost.

Celery soup

To serve hot

Add finely diced ham or top with grated cheese or, to give colour, add a few strips of red or green pepper.

To serve cold

Top with balls of soft cream cheese and paprika, stir in celery salt and a little cream or mayonnaise. This is delicious if slightly iced.

Consommé or clear soup

To serve hot

Prepare with stock cube and water. Then serve with any of the traditional additions and garnishes; tiny matchsticks (julienne) of vegetables—very fine cooked spaghetti—or wine.

5-minute borshch:

It makes a splendid basis for Borshch. To approximately 1¼ pints consommé allow 1 large cooked beetroot, a little garlic salt and a squeeze lemon juice. Grate beetroot coarsely and put into consommé with lemon juice and garlic salt. Pour into soup cups and top with soured cream, or a spoonful of cream cheese, or fresh cream.

To serve cold

See Jellied and Iced consommé recipes, page 25.

Chicken soup

To serve hot

Add interest by using one of the following:

1 Blanched shredded almonds.
2 Equal amount of asparagus or mushroom soup mixed with chicken and topped with fried bread croûtons.
3 Make a little thinner than usual then cook a small packet frozen vegetables and 1 oz. rice with it to give Chicken broth.
4 Turn it into a creamed curry soup: fry 1 small chopped onion and 1–2 teaspoons curry powder in little margarine or butter until onion is tender. Add enough chicken soup for 4 and heat or cook in usual way.
5 Top with chopped watercress.

To serve cold

Blend with little cream and mayonnaise (see page 36), top with lightly whipped cream flavoured with little grated lemon rind.

Green pea soup

To serve hot

1 The soup can be curried in same way as the preceding Chicken soup.
2 It is also excellent mixed with very fine strips of cooked ham or crisply fried snippets of bacon, and topped with croûtons of toasted bread.
3 Mix with a tomato soup. Use rather more green pea than tomato—or mix with equal quantity of mixed vegetable or celery soup.

To serve cold

Not as successful as some soups but quite palatable if a little cream is added. Top with chopped fresh mint.

Kidney soup

To serve hot

Add just a little sherry or port wine. Made rather thinner than usual this soup can be

turned into a sustaining dish if dumplings the size of an acorn are cooked in it (see recipe page 14).

This is not particularly suitable to serve cold.

Meat soups

These have very definite flavour which is inclined to predominate if mixed with other soups. They are better therefore if served by themselves. Add to them a little red wine—a garnish of cooked rice—croûtons (see page 8)—cheese straws (see page 42)—potato crisps—put on immediately before serving.

Mushroom or Cream of mushroom soup

To serve hot

Give this a little extra flavouring with mushroom ketchup or Tabasco sauce. Garnish with croûtons of fried bread and chopped parsley.

To serve cold

Add a little sherry and cream.

Onion soup

To serve hot

Top with toast or French bread and grated cheese and put under the grill for a few minutes. Onion soup can be mixed with tomato, chicken, or vegetable soups to give additional flavour.

To serve cold

A really good onion soup, if blended with a little cream and white wine, is not unlike a Vichyssoise.

Tomato soup

This makes an excellent basis for chowders (see page 31). As it is a soup so many people enjoy, it can also be served with one of the following flavourings to prevent it becoming monotonous.

To serve hot

1 Fry thinly sliced rings onion in a little margarine or butter until tender. Add to the tomato soup before serving.

2 Make rather thinner than usual and cook 2 medium grated raw carrots and add 1 oz. rice to each pint liquid for a Tomato carrot broth.

3 Pour into soup cups, top with a thick layer grated cheese and brown under grill for a moment or so.

4 Mix with celery soup and top with snippets of crisply fried bacon.

To serve cold

Blend with little cream or mayonnaise and top with freshly chopped mint.

Turtle soup

This is always improved by adding just a little sherry and often cheese straws (see page 42) are served with it.

To serve cold

Add sherry and gelatine as for consommé (see page 25) but as it is fairly gelatinous use only half the amount of powdered gelatine.

Vegetable soups

There is a variety of these—Cream of vegetable, Thick vegetable, etc., but all are generally improved if a little cream or top of the milk is added. The colour is sometimes rather dull so freshly grated carrot, diced tomato and parsley cooked for a few minutes in the soup add interest.

To serve cold

If there are pieces of vegetable in the soup it is better when sieved. Add a little cream and white wine, chill thoroughly and top with slices of lemon.

Making chowders with ready-prepared soups

Potato chowder

you will need:

1½ pints cooked packet or canned tomato, celery or chicken soup	little celery (when in season)
½ lb. potatoes, peeled	chopped parsley
1 carrot, scraped	seasoning

1 Cut all vegetables into small dice and put into hot soup.

2 Cook for 10–15 minutes until vegetables are soft but unbroken.

3 Season well and top with parsley.

4 Serve with crisp toast.

Potato and corn chowder

Ingredients as above, but use about 4 tablespoons canned or frozen corn instead of celery and carrot, plus small amount of grated onion.

Potato and fish chowder

Ingredients as above, but use 3-oz. shellfish or 6 oz. raw white fish instead of celery and carrot. Cut fish into tiny pieces and cook for about 6 minutes (allow less cooking time for shell fish). Garnish with lemon slices and cayenne or paprika.

Vegetable cheese chowder

you will need:

1¼ pints cooked packet or canned celery, asparagus or mushroom soup	1 large packet mixed frozen vegetables
	3 tablespoons milk
	4 oz. grated cheese
	paprika

1 Tip frozen vegetables into hot soup.

2 Cook until just soft, add milk and cheese and heat gently until cheese has melted. DO NOT OVERCOOK or cheese will become 'stringy'.

3 Garnish with paprika.

Fish bisque

you will need:

1½ pints cooked packet or canned tomato, celery, asparagus or mushroom soup	4 oz. shellfish or 8 oz. diced raw white fish
	seasoning
	1 hard-boiled egg
	little parsley

1 Put the fish into hot soup and cook for about 6 minutes (allow little less cooking time for shell fish).

2 Season very well.

3 Chop hard-boiled egg and parsley and sprinkle over soup before serving.

Time Savers for the Store Cupboard

All too often recipes depend on a pinch of herbs or rather unusual seasoning to make them interesting. Ready-chopped dried herbs give flavour to a soup or savoury when you haven't time to chop fresh ones—this does not mean they are better than fresh herbs but just more convenient. Since these keep well it is well worth while purchasing some, if not all of the following.

HERBS

Basil for soups and stews
Balm used in stuffings
Bay leaves for soups and stews
Borage flavouring fruit and other drinks
Caraway for cakes
Celery for pickles
Coriander for curries and cakes
Mint for fruit drinks, salads
Parsley as a stand-by when fresh parsley not obtainable
Rosemary—use a very little inside a roasting fowl when fresh not available
Sage for stuffing or savoury dishes
Thyme for soups and stuffings

SAUCES

Worcestershire sauce for Tomato juice cocktails and adding bite to savoury dishes
Tabasco sauce can also be used for the same purpose, but gives a much hotter result

Chilli sauce same use but very hot indeed
Tomato sauce for adding to certain soups and savoury dishes
Soy sauce if you like Chinese cooking: also for sour-sweet sauce

SEASONINGS

English mustard
French mustard
Salt—both table and cooking
Celery salt for giving a celery flavour that is delicious in cooking
Garlic salt a mild garlic flavour
White pepper for table use
Black pepper stronger—for cooking
Paprika a sweet Hungarian pepper for goulash, garnishes
Cayenne a more hot red pepper to be used sparingly for cooking and garnishes
Vinegar brown or white malt for general purposes, pickling
White wine vinegar for fish recipes
Red wine vinegar for stronger dishes
Also obtainable are flavoured vinegars, such as sage, tarragon and garlic

DRIED MILK

It is now possible to purchase very good quality dried milk and a tin enables you to make a home-made soup or sauce even if you are short of milk.

Hors-d'œuvre

An hors-d'œuvre creates a very pleasant beginning to a meal and these easily prepared savouries help to make a meal more of a special occasion. If you have a fairly light main course they can make the meal more sustaining.
There is a great variety of foods that can be served as hors-d'œuvre and the following chapter gives some suggestions.

Method of serving
Unless you have an hors-d'œuvre dish it is better to arrange the hors-d'œuvre on individual plates. Alternatively you can arrange a selection of ingredients on little dishes on a trolley or tray so that people can help themselves.

Size of portions

It must be remembered that an hors-d'œuvre is meant to be only the beginning or 'appetizer' to a meal so do not make the portions too large.

Adding dressings and sauces

If you are serving a salad it is usual to put a mayonnaise or French dressing on this. If you are uncertain of people's likes and dislikes, it can be served separately.

Salad hors-d'œuvre

A light salad is a very good choice, either by itself or mixed with other ingredients, and in this chapter will be found several unusual as well as favourite salads. In addition the following make a good start to the meal.

Eggs

● Hard-boil, shell, then coat with mayonnaise and garnish with strips of green or red pepper or chopped parsley and paprika. Serve on a bed of lettuce.
● Hard-boil and serve as part of a mixed hors-d'œuvre.

Fish

● Shellfish, white fish and, of course, salmon, make an excellent basis for a salad. Toss in mayonnaise and arrange on lettuce or watercress.

Chicken

● A chicken salad is rather substantial for an hors-d'œuvre but the following makes a light and interesting dish.

● Chicken and walnut salad
Add enough cream to mayonnaise to make it rather thin. To each ¼ pint mayonnaise add 2 oz. very finely chopped walnuts and 4–6 oz. finely shredded chicken. Allow to stand and serve with a garnish of watercress.

Meat

● Most meats are too substantial for hors-d'œuvre, but a salad can be served with Parma ham or pâté.

Avocado and grapefruit salad

no cooking time

you will need for 4 servings:

1–2 avocado pears	endive
green pepper	other salad plants as
grapefruit	liked
tomato	French dressing (see
watercress	page 90)

1 Cut avocado pears into slices, divide the grapefruit into sections, and finely slice the green pepper.
2 Place on the prepared salad.
3 Serve with French dressing.

Avocado salad

no cooking time

you will need for 4 servings:

3 avocado pears	2 teaspoons Tabasco
2 tomatoes	sauce
1 onion, finely chopped	lettuce
2 tablespoons oil	
1 teaspoon ground	**To garnish:**
coriander, optional	2 sliced tomatoes

1 Peel avocado pears and remove stones.
2 Peel tomatoes; chop pears and tomatoes coarsely, and stir in onion.
3 Fold fruits into blended oil, coriander and Tabasco, pile on bed of lettuce in a salad bowl and garnish with sliced tomatoes.
4 Chill if possible before serving.

Caesar salad

no cooking time

you will need for 4 servings:

½ clove garlic (optional)	2 tablespoons grated
1 lettuce	cheese (optional)
little sliced cucumber	4 anchovy fillets
2 tomatoes	mayonnaise (see page 36)
1 hard-boiled egg	bread croûtons

1 Rub round a wooden salad bowl with the garlic, then arrange lettuce in the bowl with sliced cucumber, egg and tomatoes.
2 Sprinkle with the grated cheese and top with mayonnaise, anchovy fillets and croûtons.

Princess mushrooms

cooking time   10 minutes

you will need for 4 servings:

8 oz. mushrooms	**For the filling:**
1 oz. margarine or	3 oz. margarine or
butter	butter
seasoning	2 egg yolks
	2 tablespoons finely
	grated cheese
	seasoning

1 Choose small mushrooms. Peel and separate stalks.
2 Put the mushrooms and stalks into a casserole together with seasoning and margarine.
3 Cook gently in a moderate oven (375°F.—Gas Mark 4) for 10 minutes.
4 Drain thoroughly and cool.
5 Cream margarine and add finely chopped or sieved egg yolks and cheese.
6 Season well.
7 Pipe or pile into the middle of each mushroom and decorate with the stalk.

Oriental chicken and rice salad

cooking time   20 minutes

you will need for 4 servings:

6 oz. rice	1 large tomato, skinned,
cut clove garlic, optional	seeded and chopped
3 tablespoons salad oil	1 green pepper, finely
1 tablespoon vinegar	sliced
(wine or tarragon for	2 tablespoons chopped
preference)	walnuts, optional
salt and pepper	8 oz. cooked chicken,
1 tablespoon currants	cut into bite-size
	pieces

1 Cook rice in boiling, salted water and drain very thoroughly.
2 Meanwhile rub a large bowl with garlic and in it mix together the oil, vinegar and seasoning.
3 Add the hot rice and mix thoroughly.
4 Stir in the remaining ingredients and lastly the chicken.
5 Cover and set aside in a cool place for the flavours to blend.
6 When cold transfer to a serving dish.

Rice hors-d'œuvre

cooking time   20 minutes

you will need for 4 servings:

3 oz. rice	1 teaspoon chopped
1 tablespoon oil	gherkins
1 tablespoon vinegar	1 teaspoon chopped
3–4 oz. shrimps or	chives or onion
prawns	seasoning
	lettuce

1 Cook rice in boiling, salted water until just soft and drain well.
2 To the rice add the oil, vinegar, shrimps or prawns, gherkins, chives and seasoning, and mix everything together.
3 Pile on to the lettuce and serve thoroughly chilled.

Potato salad

cooking time   20–25 minutes

you will need for 4 servings:

1 lb. potatoes	2 teaspoons finely
¼ pint mayonnaise or	chopped onion
French dressing (see	3 tablespoons finely
page 90)	chopped parsley
	seasoning

1 Cook the potatoes in salted water until just cooked, making sure that they do not become over-soft.
2 Strain and leave until just cool enough to handle—BUT NOT COLD. (The secret of a good potato salad is to mix it when warm, then serve it when very cold.)
3 Cut into neat dice and toss in the mayonnaise, adding onion, parsley and seasoning.
4 Leave until cold, then if desired garnish with a little more chopped parsley.
5 If preferred, toss in oil and vinegar instead of mayonnaise.

Variations:

Add little diced cucumber or gherkin.
Add finely chopped celery and capers.
Add finely chopped celery, diced eating apple and raisins.

Heavenly potato salad

Method and ingredients as Potato salad but add:

a little finely chopped	chopped hard-boiled
crisp bacon	eggs
a little diced celery	
and/or green pepper	**To garnish:**
	parsley and eggs

Russian salad

no cooking

you will need for 4 servings:

8 oz. cooked potatoes	4 oz. cooked turnips*
8 oz. cooked carrots	seasoning
8 oz. cooked peas	2 tablespoons oil
8 oz. runner or French	1 tablespoon vinegar
beans*	lettuce, optional
	mayonnaise (see page 36)

*Or use cooked mixed frozen vegetables

1 Cut all the vegetables into neat dice.
2 Put into a large bowl and pour over the oil and vinegar, then season well.
3 Leave for several hours, turning gently round in the dressing from time to time, so that the vegetables are not broken.
4 When ready to serve, pile on to a dish—on lettuce bed if desired—and form into pyramid.
5 Pour over just enough mayonnaise to coat.

Salad niçoise

no cooking time

you will need:

1 can tuna fish	½ teaspoon salt
1 lettuce	black pepper
1 small can anchovy	little garlic juice or
fillets	pinch garlic salt
3–4 tomatoes	little chopped fresh
2 hard-boiled eggs	herbs, chervil, parsley,
1 small green pepper or	chives, etc., or pinch
can red or green	dried herbs when out
pepper	of season
black olives	¼ pint corn oil
	2 tablespoons wine
For the vinaigrette	vinegar
dressing:	1 tablespoon tarragon
1 level teaspoon made	vinegar
mustard	1 tablespoon lemon
2 teaspoons sugar	juice

1 Drain off the oil from the tuna fish.
2 Put the lettuce into a salad bowl or arrange on a platter.
3 Put the tuna in the centre and arrange all the other ingredients round it.
4 Garnish with the pepper, cut into strips, and the olives.
5 Serve with vinaigrette dressing made as 6.
6 Mix all the seasonings and herbs together, stir in the corn oil and finally beat in the vinegar and lemon juice.

Spanish salad

no cooking

you will need for 4 servings:

4 oz. cooked rice	1 chopped red pepper
2 oz. cooked peas	seasoning
(approximately)	finely chopped garlic
1 thinly sliced tomato	clove or few chopped
2 teaspoons capers	spring onions
2 sliced gherkins	

Mix all together and toss in mayonnaise.

Stuffed apples

no cooking time

you will need for 4 servings:

4 large red apples	1 oz. walnuts
2 sticks celery	few blanched almonds
2 oz. raisins	mayonnaise (see page 36)
2 oz. stoned dates	

1 Cut the tops of the apples and carefully remove the core and a little of the pulp.
2 Mix together the chopped celery, raisins, dates, walnuts and enough mayonnaise to bind.
3 Pile into the apple cases.
4 Pipe a little mayonnaise around the edge and arrange spiked almonds on top.

Summer mould

cooking time   few minutes

you will need for 4 servings:

6 oz. button mushrooms	1 large apple, peeled
little salt	and chopped
3 tomatoes	4 oz. peeled prawns
3 tablespoons cider	2 hard-boiled eggs,
vinegar	chopped
1 tablespoon gelatine	3 sliced tomatoes
2 tablespoons hot water	

1 Sprinkle mushrooms with salt.
2 Cover with water and simmer for 3 minutes.
3 Skin and seed tomatoes, then crush tomato pulp.
4 Mix the crushed tomatoes with the vinegar.
5 Dissolve the gelatine in 2 tablespoons hot water.
6 Stir into the mixture and add water to make 1 pint.
7 Mix together the apple, prawns, mushrooms and eggs.
8 Put this mixture into the mould (individual moulds could be used if preferred).
9 Top with the sliced tomato.
10 Pour over the gelatine mixture and allow to set.
11 Serve on a bed of chopped lettuce or salad vegetables.

Tomato and ham creams

no cooking time

you will need for 4 servings:

8 tiny firm tomatoes
seasoning
1 teaspoon capers
2 teaspoons chopped
 gherkins
4 oz. ham, finely chopped

2 tablespoons cream
 cheese
1 tablespoon mayonnaise
 (see below)
lettuce
cucumber slices

1 Halve tomatoes, remove centre pulp, chop finely then mix with seasoning, capers, gherkins and ham.
2 Pile back into tomato cases.
3 Mix together cheese and mayonnaise and pile or pipe on top of each halved tomato.
4 Arrange on a bed of lettuce and garnish with slices of cucumber.

Mayonnaise

no cooking

you will need:

1 teaspoon sugar
1 teaspoon dry
 mustard
$\frac{1}{2}$ teaspoon salt
 and pinch pepper

1 egg*
approximately $\frac{1}{4}$—$\frac{1}{2}$ pint
 oil (salad, olive or
 corn)
3 tablespoons vinegar

*For a richer mayonnaise use only egg yolk

1 Combine the sugar, mustard, seasoning and egg and beat well with a rotary beater.
2 Add two-thirds of the oil VERY GRADU- ALLY, beating all the time, then stir in 1 tablespoon vinegar.
3 Add remaining one-third of the oil, beating all the time.
4 Finally mix in the remaining vinegar.

Using fruit and vegetables

Both fruit and vegetables make a very pleasant beginning to a meal; they are refreshing, not too filling and enable one to choose those foods that are in season and so at their best.

Asparagus

● Cooked or canned asparagus served with melted butter. Remember to provide finger bowls for people as it is eaten with the fingers— soup cups with a small flower floating in the cold water could be used instead.

● Serve hot or cold with hollandaise sauce (see page 90).
● Served cold with vinaigrette dressing (see page 37).
● *Au gratin:* arrange the hot asparagus in individual dishes, top with breadcrumbs and melted butter and brown under the grill. Finely grated cheese could be put on top as well.
● *Polonaise:* top cooked asparagus with crisp fried breadcrumbs, chopped hard-boiled egg, parsley and melted butter. In this method, as for *au gratin,* you will serve the asparagus with knife and fork.

Avocado pear

● Halve, remove stone and fill cavity with French dressing or with shrimps or prawns in mayonnaise (this page) or French dressing (page 90).
● Serve in a salad—see Avocado and grape- fruit salad, page 33.

Artichokes

● Cook as page 37 and serve with hollandaise sauce or hot melted butter.
● Serve cold with vinaigrette dressing (page 37). You need finger bowls, as for asparagus.
● Cook small artichokes, remove the leaves, crush the lower fleshy part of the leaves, blend with chopped hard-boiled egg, put on a bed of lettuce and top with the artichoke hearts from which you have scooped out the hairy centre. Pour over mayonnaise or vinaigrette dressing.

Note:

The fleshy leaves are left whole, to be dipped in a vinaigrette dressing, and can be eaten with the fingers. A small knife and fork will be needed for the heart.

Beans

Young French beans make a delicious salad if tossed in oil, vinegar and seasoning and garnished with chopped chives or spring onions.

Carrots

One would not serve these separately but they can make a very attractive part of an hors- d'œuvre. If young use raw, grated. If older, dice and cook.

Chicory
Cook lightly in lemon and salt flavoured water.
Serve with a cheese sauce (see page 89).

Leeks
Young leeks can be cooked and used as asparagus.

Mushrooms
Cooked or diced raw mushrooms can be put in a mixed hors-d'œuvre or served as a salad with vinaigrette dressing (see below).

Tomatoes
● When tomatoes are at their best one of the simplest hors-d'œuvre is to slice and toss them in oil and vinegar and seasoning, adding a little garlic or chopped chives or spring onions. Serve with a garnish of watercress as a salad.

● They can be stuffed with eggs, fish, meat, cottage cheese and served raw or lightly cooked.

Artichokes with vinaigrette dressing

cooking time   30—40 minutes

you will need for 4 servings:
4 globe artichokes
vinaigrette dressing
    (see below)

1 Wash artichokes and cut off the stems and the outer layer of leaves.
2 Simmer steadily for 30–40 minutes until tender.
3 Drain well and allow to cool.
4 Serve on small plates with the dressing.

Vinaigrette dressing

you will need:

2 dessertspoons vinegar (wine vinegar, cider vinegar or tarragon vinegar)	5 dessertspoons olive oil good pinch salt pepper to taste

Mix all the ingredients thoroughly together.

Fish hors-d'œuvre

On the following pages are suggestions for serving smoked or cooked shellfish as an hors-d'œuvre. Good choice for the busy cook for they need little cooking or elaborate preparation, and yet give a touch of luxury and interest to a meal. Other fish also make excellent hors-d'œuvre or light savouries.

Anchovies
● Top slices of fried bread or toast with chopped hard-boiled egg and anchovy fillets. Spread toast with anchovy butter (see page 55) before topping with the egg and fillets. Serve on a bed of lettuce or watercress.

● This is also a good savoury to end a meal. Take the tops off firm tomatoes, scoop out the centre pulp, chop finely and mix with chopped anchovy fillets and hard-boiled egg. Pile this mixture back into tomato cases. Serve on a bed of lettuce with sliced cucumber.

● Use the same recipe as for Scotch woodcock but serve the egg—when cold—on a bed of salad (see page 47).

● Rollmop or Bismarck herrings can be served as part of a mixed hors-d'œuvre or as a separate salad. Garnish with plenty of sliced onion, gherkins and serve with diced beetroot, diced dessert apple, lettuce, etc.

● The canned herring tit-bits can also be served as a salad.

Sardines, Sild, Pilchards
● These canned fish are best as part of mixed hors-d'œuvre or served separately as the basis of a salad. Serve with hard-boiled egg, watercress, etc.

● Fill patty case with the mashed fish. Top with chopped hard-boiled egg.

Prawns, Shrimps, Scampi, Lobster, Crab
● Prawns and shrimps are excellent in cocktails —see page 39—or lobster and crab could be used instead.

● Fried—the larger scampi are generally used for this. Coat with egg and crumbs and fry for a few minutes only in hot fat. Drain and serve with tartare sauce, page 91. Frozen scampi should be defrosted, dried well then coated.

● Meunière—toss the fish in hot butter until just cooked (in the case of the frozen uncooked scampi) or just hot. Lift on to a hot dish, then add a little lemon juice, chopped parsley and seasoning to the butter and continue heating until golden brown. Pour over the fish and garnish with lemon, parsley.

● Serve all shellfish as the base for salads with mayonnaise (see page 36).

Oysters

Serve on half the shell with lemon and cayenne pepper—some people like a little vinegar as well. Serve with brown bread and butter.

Serving smoked fish

There is a great variety of smoked fish today that can be served as an hors-d'œuvre or, if a more generous quantity is given, as a light savoury.

Smoked eel

Allow approximately 2 inches per person or 3–4 pieces of fillet. Remove the black skin and serve on a bed of lettuce with wedges of lemon, accompanied by horseradish sauce (see page 90) and brown bread and butter.

Smoked trout

Can be served as smoked eel.

Smoked salmon

Serve with lemon, paprika or cayenne and brown bread and butter.

Smoked sprats

As smoked salmon.

Uncooked kipper fillets

Can be served as an inexpensive substitute for smoked salmon. Marinade in a little oil and vinegar, with pepper and a little chopped onion and leave for several hours.

Antipasto

no cooking

you will need:

fillets of anchovies	pickled onions
rolled anchovies	hard-boiled eggs
small mushrooms—cooked in a very little vinegar	pimentos
	sliced tomatoes
	sardines
pickled beetroot, cut into tiny shapes	olives—both green and black

Arrange these either on individual plates or on one large serving dish, so that the colours form as attractive a picture as possible.

Scampi meunière

cooking time   about 6 minutes

you will need for 4 servings:

1 large packet frozen scampi	seasoning
3 oz. butter	1 tablespoon chopped parsley
little lemon juice	

1 Allow scampi to defrost sufficiently to separate easily.
2 Heat the butter in a frying pan and cook the scampi for about 4–5 minutes.
3 Lift out the fish and put on to hot dish.
4 Add lemon juice and seasoning to butter and cook until brown in colour. This takes only about 1–2 minutes, and care must be taken that it does not darken too much.
5 Add parsley and pour over the fish.

Mock smoked salmon

no cooking

you will need:

frozen kipper fillets	little vinegar
little oil	seasoning

1 Let kipper fillets defrost, then put on a flat dish (allowing one per person).
2 Cover with a little oil, vinegar and seasoning, particularly a good shaking of pepper.
3 Leave for several hours, lift out of the dressing and serve in the same way as smoked salmon with lemon and brown bread and butter.

Tabasco cocktail sauce

no cooking

you will need:

½ pint tomato ketchup
½–1 teaspoon Tabasco
  sauce
2 tablespoons lemon
  juice
¼ teaspoon salt

1 tablespoon horse-
  radish cream
2 tablespoons finely
  chopped celery
1 teaspoon grated
  onion, optional

Mix all ingredients and chill before serving.

White fish cocktails

no cooking

you will need for 4 servings:

8–12 oz. cooked fish*
Tabasco cocktail sauce
  (see above)

little lettuce
slices of lemon

*This can be a mixture of white fish—tuna—salmon—or use cooked white fish and little shellfish

1 Flake the cooked fish.
2 Shred the lettuce finely, enough to be eaten with fork or spoon.
3 Blend the fish with enough of the cocktail sauce to moisten well.
4 Arrange lettuce in glasses or on dishes and top with the fish.
5 Garnish with slices of lemon.

Note:

The stronger tasting cocktail sauce is more suitable for this cocktail as it gives greater interest, colour, etc. to white fish.

Prawn cocktail

no cooking

you will need for 4 servings:

picked prawns or shrimps
lemon
lettuce
For the cocktail sauce:
3 tablespoons thick
  mayonnaise (see
  page 36)
1 tablespoon tomato
  ketchup, or thick
  tomato purée, or
  skinned tomatoes

1 tablespoon Worcester-
  shire sauce
2 tablespoons full cream
  or evaporated milk
seasoning
little celery salt (or
  chopped celery)
little finely chopped
  onion (optional)
little lemon juice

To make the sauce:

1 Mix all the sauce ingredients together, and taste to check seasoning and lemon juice.

To make the cocktail:

2 This can be arranged in glasses or flat small dishes. Shred the lettuce very finely, so it can be eaten with a spoon or small fork.
3 Top with the prawns or shrimps and cover with the sauce.
4 Garnish with lemon.
5 Serve as cold as possible.

Anchovy potatoes

no cooking

you will need for 4 servings:

6 cooked new potatoes
2 oz. butter or
  margarine
few drops lemon juice
1 teaspoonful anchovy
  essence

To garnish:
filleted anchovies
watercress

1 Cream the butter or margarine, add the lemon juice and anchovy essence.
2 Cut the potatoes in halves and pipe a large rosette of the anchovy mixture on top of each half.
3 Decorate with tiny pieces of anchovy and sprigs of watercress.

Stuffed peppers

cooking time   30 minutes

you will need for 4 servings:

4 green peppers
1 clove garlic
4 large tomatoes
2 tablespoons oil

1 can anchovy fillets
4 oz. cooked rice
little parsley
seasoning

1 Cut tops of peppers and remove core and seeds.
2 Cook for 5 minutes in boiling salted water.
3 Chop the garlic and skin and chop the tomatoes.
4 Fry in the hot oil.
5 Chop the anchovies.
6 Add rice, anchovies, parsley and seasoning to the tomato mixture.
7 Fill peppers with this mixture, and put back the tops.
8 Put into a greased dish and cover with greased paper.
9 Bake for 25 minutes in a moderately hot oven (400°F—Gas Mark 5).
10 Serve with tomato sauce (see page 91).

Egg dishes

Because an egg is a light and easily digestible food, egg dishes are ideal at the beginning of the meal. You can serve small omelettes (see page 57), hard-boiled eggs in salads, as well as savoury eggs (see recipes below).

Egg florentine

cooking time   30 minutes

you will need for 4 servings:

1½ lb. spinach	seasoning
½ oz. butter	4 poached eggs
1 tablespoon cornflour	
¼ pint milk	**To garnish:**
3–4 tablespoons cream	toast
pinch nutmeg	

1 Wash and cook the spinach in the usual way then rub through a sieve.
2 Make a sauce with the butter, cornflour and milk then stir in the spinach.
3 Add the cream, nutmeg and seasoning to taste.
4 Reheat, then put in four cocottes or individual serving dishes and carefully place a poached egg on the top of each.
5 Decorate with triangles of toast.

Stuffed eggs with martinique dressing

no cooking

you will need for 4 servings:

mayonnaise (see page 36)	**For the dressing:**
pinch cayenne	3 fl. oz. corn oil
4 hard-boiled eggs	1 fl. oz. vinegar
2 large tomatoes	¼ teaspoon salt
1 oz. cheese	1 teaspoon sugar
seasoning	1 teaspoon chopped parsley
To garnish:	a little chopped green pepper
watercress	

1 Make mayonnaise, adding pinch cayenne to ingredients.
2 Remove a small piece from the top of each egg and scoop out the yoke.
3 Cut the tomatoes in halves and remove the pulp.
4 Place egg white in the tomato halves.
5 Mix together yolks, tomato pulp, cheese and seasoning to taste and use sufficient mayonnaise to bind.

6 Pile the egg mixture into the eggs and garnish with watercress.
7 To prepare dressing, put corn oil, vinegar, salt and sugar into a screw top jar and shake well; add parsley and pepper.
8 Serve with the stuffed eggs.

Meat hors-d'œuvre

Most meat is too heavy to serve as an hors-d'œuvre but the following are light, unusual and very delicious:

Parma or smoked ham

Can be served with slices of ripe melon, dessert or canned figs or a ripe dessert pear. Do not put sugar on the melon but offer sugar and a little cayenne separately.

Salami

Choose a variety of salami and serve very thin slices on crisp lettuce.

Garlic sausages

Very good with tomato salads and green salad.

Chopped liver

cooking time   5 minutes

you will need for 4 servings:

8 oz. calf's or chicken's liver	1½ oz. melted fat (chicken fat is ideal)
1 medium onion	1 hard-boiled egg
seasoning	

1 Fry the liver and chopped onion in the fat for about 5 minutes.
2 Lift out and chop both on a board very finely or put through a mincer.
3 Add seasoning.
4 Moisten with a little fat from the frying pan.
5 Arrange on a dish and cover with chopped hard-boiled egg.

Make Your Own Pâté

A pâté is probably one of the most popular hors-d'œuvre and, although you can buy very good pâté, a home-made one is both simple to make and particularly delicious to eat.

Crème à la Grecque

no cooking

you will need for 4 servings:

½ lb. smoked cod's roe	juice 1 lemon
4–6 oz. unsalted butter	1 tomato

1 Skin the cod's roe.
2 Cream the butter.
3 Pound the roe, adding butter, lemon juice, tomato juice and pulp.
4 When very light and creamy serve with black olives and hot toast or water biscuits.

Fish pâté

cooking time   20 minutes

you will need for 4 servings:

approximately 1 lb. salt smoked cod's roe	pepper very little cream (optional)
clove garlic, crushed	
2 oz. butter	

1 Remove the skin from the cod's roe and put into a basin.
2 Add the very finely crushed garlic (garlic salt could be used instead), the butter and pepper.
3 Blend together very thoroughly and add the cream.
4 Cook very gently in another dish of cold water for about 20 minutes in a moderate oven (375°F.—Gas Mark 4), covering the top so it does not dry.

Creamed liver pâté

cooking time   55 minutes

you will need:

For the sauce:	
1 oz. margarine	1 teaspoon cinnamon
2 oz. flour	1 teaspoon ginger
½ pint milk	2 eggs
	¼ pint cream

8 oz. bacon, either shoulder or middle rashers	**To cover the pâté while cooking:**
1 lb. lamb or pork liver	4 oz. bacon rashers
½ teaspoon sugar	**To garnish:**
2 teaspoons salt	gherkins, lemon, parsley, hot toast
pinch black pepper	

1 Heat margarine, stir in flour, cook for 1 minute.
2 Gradually add milk.
3 Bring to the boil.
4 Cook until thickened.
5 Mince bacon and liver until it is very smooth. Stir into sauce.
6 Add all other ingredients.
7 Press mixture firmly into a greased shallow fireproof dish.
8 Arrange the bacon rashers across the top.
9 Stand in a water bath (another dish, partly filled with cold water) and cook for 45 minutes in the centre of a very moderate oven (350°F.—Gas Mark 3).
10 Allow to cool, then serve garnished with gherkin, lemon, parsley and hot toast.

Variations:

For a coarser pâté put the meat and bacon through a coarse mincer and allow only ⅓ pint of milk.

For a less creamy pâté omit or reduce the cream.

For a chicken liver pâté use half the quantity of bacon to the quantity of chicken livers.

For a pâté with more bite add chopped gherkins and a little chopped onion.

End-of-Meal Savouries

A number of dishes can be served at the end of a meal but remember that this is not a main course and portions, therefore, should be small; a Welsh rarebit which would normally serve 4 people will be plenty for 8 if used as a light supper savoury at the end of a meal. Here are some suggestions.

Cheese

● Toasted on bread—put slices of Gruyère or

Cheddar cheese on hot buttered toast and brown under a grill.

● As one of the various kinds of Welsh rarebit. A Buck rarebit is a little substantial but the other varieties are all extremely good.

● As a fried savoury such as cheese aigrettes or cheese fritters (see below).

● As a soufflé (see page 61).

● As a cold dish—cheese mousse (page 44).

● A really creamy Camembert cheese is delicious if slightly iced and served with crisp lettuce and biscuits or bread.

● To give a combination of sweet and savoury —serve a cheese cake (page 44).

Bacon

● You will find a number of classic bacon savouries on page 64 and any of these make a very satisfying end to the meal.

Mushrooms

● Fry mushrooms and serve on fried bread or toast—a favourite after-dinner savoury.

● Vary by sprinkling grated cheese over them just before serving or spread the toast with a soft pâté rather than butter.

Fish

● Sardines on hot buttered toast can be varied by sprinkling with chopped parsley and grated cheese. They can also be put on top of a curry-flavoured butter (see page 55).

● Cod's roe can be fried with bacon and served on fingers of fried bread or toast.

● Soft herring roes can be steamed with butter, seasoning, and a little milk or cream between two plates over a pan of hot water. Or they can be fried in butter or margarine, or simmered in a little milk. They are then drained, put on hot buttered toast and garnished with cayenne or paprika.

Savouries with cheese

Cheese straws

cooking time   7 minutes

you will need:

4 oz. plain flour	2½ oz. butter
salt and cayenne	2 oz. grated cheese
little dry mustard	1 egg yolk

1 Sieve the flour, seasoning and mustard together, rub in the butter.

2 Add the cheese and bind with the egg yolk. If necessary add a little water as well.

3 Roll out firmly and cut into thin fingers.

4 Use a little of the pastry to make circles, so that when cooked the cheese straws can be threaded through these.

5 Brush with a very little egg white to give them a gloss.

6 Bake on lightly greased tins in a hot oven (450°F.—Gas Mark 7) for approximately 7 minutes.

7 Allow to cool slightly on the tin as the mixture is brittle and could very easily break.

Variation:

Cheese twists

Make pastry as above, roll out into a thin oblong strip and cut in halves. Spread one half with yeast extract and place the other half on top. Roll lightly together, cut into ¼-inch strips, twist and bake as above for about 10 minutes.

Cheese whirls

Make pastry as for straws, roll into a thin oblong, spread with yeast extract, roll up like a Swiss roll and cut into slices. Cook as from step 5 for about 10 minutes.

Cheese and tomato whirls

Make pastry as above, roll out into an oblong, spread with 2½ oz. can tomato paste, roll up from the long side and cut into ¼-inch slices. Cook as step 6 for 12 minutes.

Cheese aigrettes 1

cooking time   12 minutes

you will need for 4 servings:

⅛ pint corn oil	pinch of salt
¼ pint water	2 eggs
2½ oz. plain flour and ½ oz. cornflour, or 3 oz. plain flour	2 oz. Cheddar cheese pinch cayenne

1 Heat corn oil and water to boiling point in a saucepan.

2 Remove from the heat, add flour, cornflour and salt sifted together.

3 Mix well, return to the heat and cook until the mixture forms a ball and leaves the sides of the pan clean.

4 Remove from the heat, cool a little, then beat in the eggs one at a time.

5 Lastly add the grated cheese and cayenne.

6 Drop teaspoonsful into corn oil heated moderately and fry till well puffed and golden brown.

Variations:

Cheese and tomato aigrettes
Use $\frac{1}{4}$ pint tomato juice in place of water.

Cheese and bacon aigrettes
Use 1 oz. finely diced, cooked bacon as well as the cheese.

Savoury aigrettes
Use 1 teaspoon yeast extract with the water. Omit the salt.

Cheese aigrettes 2

cooking time   12 minutes

you will need for 4 servings:

1 oz. butter	pinch salt and cayenne
$\frac{1}{8}$ pint water	$1\frac{1}{2}$ oz. grated cheese
2 oz. plain flour	(mixed Cheddar and
2 eggs	Parmesan)

1 Bring butter and water to boiling point.

2 Toss in all the flour at once and beat until smooth.

3 Cool, then add the eggs gradually, beating the mixture very well after each addition.

4 Stir in the cheese and seasoning.

5 Drop small teaspoons of the mixture into a pan of hot deep fat (350°F.) and fry to a golden brown, taking 7–10 minutes.

6 Drain and serve hot, sprinkled with a little grated cheese.

Variations:

Nutty cheese aigrettes
Add $\frac{1}{2}$ oz. salted chopped almonds to the mixture together with the grated cheese.
Variations given above with Cheese aigrettes 1 can also be used with this recipe.

Cheese puffs 1

cooking time   10 minutes

you will need for 4 servings:

3 oz. margarine or butter	$3\frac{1}{2}$ oz. Cheddar cheese, grated
$\frac{1}{4}$ pint water	pepper
4 oz. plain flour	pinch cayenne
pinch salt	$\frac{1}{4}$ teaspoon made mustard
3 eggs	oil for frying
	parsley

1 Boil water in a saucepan; add butter. When melted, remove from heat and add flour and salt all at once.

2 Return to the heat and beat until mixture forms a soft ball and no longer sticks to the sides of the pan.

3 Cool.

4 Beat in eggs one at a time, then work in 3 oz. of cheese, the pepper and cayenne and mustard.

5 Put teaspoons of the mixture into deep, hot oil and cook for about 7 minutes until well puffed out and firm to the touch.

6 Drain and serve hot, sprinkled with remaining $\frac{1}{2}$ oz. grated cheese.

7 Garnish with parsley.

Cheese puffs 2

cooking time   3–4 minutes

you will need for 4 servings:

4 oz. finely grated Cheddar cheese	$\frac{1}{2}$ teaspoon salt
pinch cayenne	1 egg
	fat for frying

1 Mix the cheese, seasoning, and stir in the beaten egg yolk.

2 Fold in the stiffly beaten egg white and shape lightly in the hands into small balls.

3 Fry a few at a time in hot, deep fat (350°F. approximately or until a cube of bread turns brown in 1 minute) to a golden brown, taking 3–4 minutes.

4 Drain and serve as a savoury snack or on cocktail sticks for a party.

Variations:

Use 3 oz. grated cheese and 1 oz. chopped nuts.
Use 3 oz. grated cheese and 1 oz. diced ham.
Use 3 oz. grated cheese and 1 oz. very finely chopped green pepper.

English monkey

cooking time   few minutes

you will need for 4 servings :

1 oz. butter	mustard
$\frac{1}{4}$ pint evaporated milk	Worcestershire sauce
2 oz. breadcrumbs	4 slices toast
4 oz. grated cheese	1 tomato
1 egg	

1 Heat butter in a pan, add milk and bread-crumbs.
2 When very hot add the grated cheese and beaten egg.
3 Season well, adding a little made mustard and few drops of Worcestershire sauce.
4 Stir together until thick and creamy.
5 Pour on to toast with sliced tomato.

Lemon cheese cake

cooking time $1\frac{1}{4}$ hours

you will need for 4 servings :

For lining baking dish:	2 large or 3 small eggs
4 good tablespoons cornflakes	grated rind 1 lemon
little margarine	juice 1 lemon
	12 oz. cream or cottage cheese
For the filling:	2 tablespoons cream or evaporated milk*
3 oz. margarine	
3 oz. sugar	

1 Crush the cornflakes finely.
2 Rub the dish with margarine and press most of the cornflakes against this.
3 Cream the margarine and sugar, separate the eggs and add the egg yolks and the lemon rind. Then work in the cheese, the cream* and lemon juice until the mixture forms a really smooth consistency.
4 Fold in the stiffly beaten egg whites.
5 Put into the cornflake-lined dish and sprinkle the remaining cornflakes as a border round the cheese cake.
6 Bake for approximately $1\frac{1}{4}$ hours in a very slow oven until set (250—275°F.—Gas Mark 1–2).

*The cream is incorporated with the lemon juice and gives a softer and more delicate cheese cake. For a firmer consistency to cut into squares for a party, omit the cream

Piquant cheese crunchies

no cooking time

you will need :

bread slices	yeast extract
a little butter	cornflakes
cream cheese	

1 Butter the bread and sandwich slices together with yeast extract.
2 Cut into neat fingers or cubes, spread outside with soft cream cheese, then roll in the crisp, crushed cornflakes.

Tomato cheese moulds

no cooking time

you will need for 4 servings :

$\frac{1}{4}$ pint tomato juice	1 teaspoon chopped parsley
4 oz. cream cheese or grated cheese	1 teaspoon chopped gherkins
2 teaspoons powdered gelatine	seasoning
4 tablespoons hot water	

1 Beat tomato juice very gradually into cheese until mixture is smooth.
2 Dissolve the gelatine in the hot water.
3 Add to cheese with seasoning, parsley and gherkins.
4 Pour into tiny moulds and turn out when set. Serve with salad.

Cheese mousse

cooking time   10 minutes

you will need :

1 oz. butter	1 heaped teaspoon mustard
1 oz. flour	
$\frac{1}{4}$ pint water	pinch salt and cayenne pepper
$\frac{1}{4}$ pint evaporated milk	
4 oz. Cheddar cheese	2 eggs
1 heaped teaspoon tomato purée	1 heaped teaspoon powdered gelatine

1 Prepare a 5-inch soufflé case by tying a wide double band of greaseproof paper round the outside so that it extends above the rim.
2 Melt the butter in a pan, stir in the flour and cook for a minute.
3 Add the water and milk gradually, bring to the boil and boil for one minute, stirring well.
4 Add the pieces of cheese, seasonings, tomato purée, egg yolks, and cook for another two minutes until smooth.
5 Soften the gelatine in 1 tablespoon cold water and dissolve in 2 tablespoons boiling water.
6 Add to the cheese mixture and allow to cool.
7 When just beginning to stiffen fold in the stiffly beaten egg whites.
8 Cool, stirring occasionally.

9 Pour into the soufflé case and put in a cool place to set.

10 Serve with a lettuce salad tossed in French dressing.

Celery and cheese soufflé

cooking time   33—43 minutes

you will need for 4 servings:

2 oz. butter	$\frac{1}{4}$ pint milk
2 oz. flour	4 eggs
1 can celery soup*	seasoning
or mushroom or	4 oz. grated cheese
tomato or chicken	

*If using condensed soup, add little more milk

1 Melt butter in saucepan, stir in flour and cook steadily for a minute.

2 Add celery soup and milk, bring to boil and cook for 2—3 minutes.

3 Allow to cool slightly.

4 Separate eggs, add beaten egg yolks, seasoning and cheese.

5 Whisk egg whites until thick and fold into mixture.

6 Pour into a 7 inch greased soufflé or pie dish and bake in a hot oven (400°F.—Gas Mark 5) for 30—40 minutes.

7 Serve at once.

Cheese soufflé

cooking time   approximately 30 minutes

you will need for 4 servings:

1 oz. butter	4 eggs, or 3 yolks and
1 oz. flour	4 whites
$\frac{1}{4}$ pint milk	4 oz. cheese, finely
seasoning	grated

1 Make a thick sauce with the butter, flour and milk.

2 Add seasoning and beat in yolks and cheese.

3 Fold in the stiffly beaten egg whites.

4 Put into greased 6—7 inch soufflé dish (with a 6 inch soufflé dish put a band of buttered paper round the top to support the mixture as it rises).

5 Bake in the centre of a moderately hot oven (400°F.—Gas Mark 5) for approximately 30 minutes.

6 Serve at once.

Variations:

For a more creamy result add 4 tablespoons of cream or extra milk to the sauce.

For a sharper result use nearly all Parmesan cheese. Use 3 oz. finely flaked smoked haddock and 2 oz. grated cheese.

10 ways with Welsh rarebit

A Welsh rarebit or 'rabbit' is a delicious tasty cheese snack that can form a complete meal, particularly if served with a really good salad, for the amount of cheese used in it is sufficiently high to produce a nourishing as well as appetising savoury.

Although this makes an excellent choice for a main savoury dish, it is one of the classic after-dinner savouries and, if serving it at the end of a meal, you'll find that the following quantities will be enough for twice the portions since only a small slice is offered. With every recipe you use for Welsh rarebit, be very careful not to over-cook the cheese in the mixture, otherwise it will be stringy and tough instead of creamy and delicious. Have the grill piping hot so that the mixture bubbles and browns quickly.

It is well worth while making a large quantity of the Welsh rarebit mixture and keeping the surplus in a jar in a cold place.

Welsh rarebit

cooking time   12 minutes

you will need for 8 after-dinner servings*:

1 oz. butter	pepper
1 oz. flour	8 oz. Cheddar cheese
$\frac{1}{4}$ pint milk	1 tablespoon beer or ale
1 teaspoon made	4—6 slices of buttered
mustard	toast
salt	

1 Heat the butter in a saucepan, stir in the flour and cook steadily for several minutes, then gradually add the cold milk.

2 Bring to the boil and cook until smooth and thick.

3 Add the mustard, salt and pepper, most of the cheese, and the beer.

(continued on next page)

*This gives 4 portions as a main savoury, or can be cut into about 32 bite-size cocktail savouries

4 Heat steadily, without boiling too quickly, until the cheese has melted.
5 Spread over the hot buttered toast, sprinkle with the remaining cheese and brown under a hot grill.
6 Serve with green salad and French dressing (see page 90).

Variations:

Creamy Welsh rarebit
Ingredients and method as for Welsh rarebit, but use processed or Dutch cheese instead of Cheddar cheese.

Welsh rarebit with a 'bite'
Ingredients as for Welsh rarebit, but use 6 oz. Lancashire and 2 oz. Parmesan cheese instead of 8 oz. Cheddar cheese. Method as for Welsh rarebit.

Eggy Welsh rarebit
Ingredients and method as for Welsh rarebit, but add a well beaten egg or egg yolk after stage 4.

Soufflé Welsh rarebit
Ingredients and method as for Welsh rarebit, but add 2 egg yolks and finally 2 stiffly beaten egg whites after stage 4.

Tomato Welsh rarebit
Ingredients and method as for Welsh rarebit, but use ¼ pint tomato juice or purée instead of milk.

Celery Welsh rarebit
Ingredients and method as for Welsh rarebit, but use either canned celery hearts or cooked celery. Put the hot celery on buttered toast and use celery stock instead of milk in the mixture.

Corn rarebit
Ingredients and method as for Welsh rarebit, but add approximately 4 oz. cooked corn after stage 3. A little corn stock can be used in place of some of the milk.

Buck rarebit
Ingredients and method as Welsh rarebit, but top each portion with a poached egg.

York rarebit
Ingredients and method as Welsh rarebit, but put a thick slice of cooked ham on each piece of toast and cover with the cheese mixture.

Fish and meat savouries

Angels on horseback

cooking time   few minutes

you will need for 4 after-dinner servings*:

4 large or 8 small oysters	squeeze lemon juice
seasoning	4 long rashers bacon

1 Season the oysters and add lemon juice.
2 Wrap a rasher of bacon round each oyster securing with a cocktail stick (if using small oysters, cut the rashers of bacon in halves).
3 Cook under the grill until the bacon is crisp and brown. Do not over-cook as this toughens the oysters.
4 Serve on hot buttered toast.

*Or 8 cocktail savouries

Canapés Diane

cooking time   few minutes

you will need for 4 after-dinner servings*:

4 chicken livers	4 rashers streaky bacon
seasoning	8 tiny toast fingers
squeeze lemon juice	

1 Cut chicken livers into halves.
2 Season and flavour with lemon juice.
3 Cut each rasher of bacon into halves.
4 Wrap each chicken liver in half rasher and secure with a cocktail stick.
5 Grill until bacon is crisp and brown.
6 Serve on pieces of hot buttered toast.

*Or 8 cocktail savouries

Devils on horseback

cooking time   few minutes

you will need for 4 servings:

8 large juicy cooked prunes	8 toast fingers butter
4 long rashers bacon	paprika

1 Stone the prunes, cut each rasher of bacon into halves and wrap round the prunes, securing with cocktail sticks.
2 Cook under the grill until the bacon is crisp and brown.
3 Serve on toast dusted with paprika.
4 If wished, a little liver pâté (see page 41) can be inserted into the centre of the prunes.

Little devils on horseback

cooking time   few minutes

you will need for 4 after-dinner servings*:

4 rashers long streaky   12 anchovy fillets
   bacon, preferably   12 squares hot buttered
   green (unsmoked)   toast

1 Divide each rasher of bacon into 3.
2 Remove the rind.
3 Put an anchovy fillet on each piece, roll firmly and secure with cocktail stick.
4 Grill until crisp and golden brown.
5 Put on to squares of hot buttered toast.
     *Or 12 cocktail savouries

Breton fingers

cooking time   few minutes

you will need for 4 servings:

1 small tin sardines in oil   little margarine or
½ teacup breadcrumbs   butter, if necessary
seasoning   ½ teaspoon made
1 teaspoon Worcester-   mustard
   shire sauce   4 slices buttered toast
3 oz. Cheddar cheese,
   grated   **To garnish:**
                    1 tomato

1 Mash the sardines very well and season.
2 Mix the oil from the sardine tin with the breadcrumbs, seasoning, Worcestershire sauce and cheese. If there is not sufficient oil to give a soft mixture then add a little margarine or butter and cream well.
4 Spread the mashed sardines on the slices of toast and cover with the crumb mixture.
5 Put under a hot grill for a few minutes until crisp and golden brown. Garnish with small pieces of tomato, and serve hot or cold.
If serving hot the fingers can be prepared earlier and just heated in oven.

Shrimp toast

cooking time   few minutes

you will need for 4 servings:

4 oz. picked shrimps   8 toast fingers
2 oz. butter   little nutmeg
seasoning

1 Chop the shrimps and bind with 1½ oz. of the butter and seasoning.
2 Use the rest of the butter to spread on the toast the moment it is cooked.

3 Cover with the shrimp butter.
4 Top with little grated or powdered nutmeg.
5 Heat for a few minutes under the grill.

Scotch woodcock

cooking time   few minutes

you will need for 4 after-dinner servings*:

4 small slices of bread   seasoning
butter   little milk
3–4 eggs   8 fillets anchovy

1 Toast the bread and butter, having removed any crusts.
2 Beat the eggs with the seasoning and a very little milk, and scramble in the hot butter. Put on the hot toast.
3 Top with anchovy fillets arranged on each portion.
     *For a supper snack double the egg quantity and use large slices of toast

Bengal canapés

cooking time   12 minutes

you will need for 4 servings:

For the sauce: 1 tablespoon cream
½ oz. margarine   2 tablespoons sweet
½ oz. flour   chutney or finely
¼ pint milk   chopped pickles
seasoning   2 tablespoons grated
                  cheese
4 slices bread
butter or margarine   **To garnish:**
4 oz. cooked ham   parsley and tomato

1 To make the sauce, heat the margarine, stir in the flour and cook for 2–3 minutes, then gradually add the milk, bring to the boil and cook until thickened.
2 Season well.
3 Toast or fry the bread, remove crusts and butter.
4 Chop the ham finely and heat for several minutes in the white sauce, adding the cream.
5 Spread over the toast, then add the chutney.
6 Cover with grated cheese and put under a hot grill for a few minutes until crisp and golden brown.
7 Garnish with parsley and strips of tomato.

Variations:

Use flaked smoked haddock in place of ham.
Use finely diced cooked liver in place of ham.

Devilled mushrooms and eggs

cooking time   few minutes

you will need for 4 servings:

2 oz. butter
4 oz. mushrooms, sliced
good pinch curry powder
½–1 teaspoon made
   mustard

1 teaspoon Worcester-
   shire sauce
1 teaspoon mushroom
   ketchup
3 hard-boiled eggs
4 rounds toast

1 Heat the butter.
2 Toss the mushrooms in this, then add all the flavourings.
3 Mix in the quartered hard-boiled eggs.
4 Heat and serve at once on toast.

Savoury choux

Choux pastry

you will need:

¼ pint water
1 oz. margarine or
   butter
3 oz. flour (plain or
   self-raising)

2 whole eggs and yolk of
   1 egg or 3 small eggs
pinch salt, pepper,
   mustard

1 Put the water, margarine or butter and seasonings into a saucepan.
2 Heat gently until the margarine or butter has melted.
3 Stir in the flour.
4 Return the pan to a low heat and cook very gently but thoroughly stirring all the time, until the mixture is dry enough to form a ball and leave the pan clean.
5 Remove the pan from the heat and gradually add the well beaten eggs. Do this slowly to produce a perfectly smooth mixture.
6 Allow to cool, then use as individual recipes.

Bun cases

cooking time   35–40 minutes

for 4 servings:

1 There are several ways of making bun cases from choux paste. Either
  a grease and flour individual patty tins and put in a spoonful of the mixture or,
  b pile some of the mixture on to well greased and floured baking trays or,
  c put the mixture into piping bags and force through a large plain pipe on to floured and greased baking tray.
2 If you have a deep tin which can be put right over the cases while in the oven, this will help to give a better shape to the buns. The tin should be light in weight and several inches high to allow room for the buns to rise.
3 Put the tray of cakes into the centre of a hot oven (450°F.—Gas Mark 7) for 35 minutes if uncovered, 40 minutes if covered. Reduce the heat for the last 20 minutes to 400°F.—Gas Mark 5.
4 The buns should be a pale gold in colour and feel very firm and crisp. If you find there is some uncooked pastry in the centre of the buns, remove this and return the buns to the oven for a few minutes to dry. The oven should be cool.
5 Cool the buns gradually and away from a draught.
6 For after-dinner savouries or cocktails use only ½ teaspoons of the mixture and you will find these need only approximately 25 minutes baking.
7 Fill as suggested on page 48.

Éclair cases

cooking time   25 minutes

you will need:

choux pastry (see
   recipe left)

1 Pipe the mixture into finger shapes on well greased and floured baking trays or put into greased and floured finger tins.
2 Bake, without covering, in the centre of a hot oven (450°F.—Gas Mark 7) for 25 minutes.
3 Fill as suggested below.

12 ways of filling savoury choux

Cheese

Make a really thick cheese sauce with 1 oz. butter, 1 oz. flour, ½ pint milk, seasoning, 4 oz. cheese. Add a little whipped cream or mayonnaise. Put into éclair or bun case and dust tops with grated cheese and chopped parsley.

Sardine
Fill with mashed sardines and chopped hard-boiled egg yolks.

Vegetable
Fill with thick cheese sauce (see Cheese filling) mixed with cooked vegetables.

Prawns, shrimp or fish
Make a thick white sauce with 1 oz. flour, 1 oz. butter, ⅓ pint milk. Add seasoning and approximately 4 oz. chopped prawns, shrimps or flaked cooked fish.

Chicken
Make a thick white sauce (see page 91) but in place of all milk use a little milk and chicken stock. Add approximately 6 oz. finely diced chicken.

Harlequin
Blend diced red and green peppers, tomatoes, cucumber and chopped hard-boiled egg with thick mayonnaise.

Salmon
Blend flaked, cooked or canned salmon with thick mayonnaise.

Ham
Blend finely chopped ham with either thick white sauce (see page 92), mayonnaise or scrambled egg.

Egg
Blend lightly scrambled egg with a little cream and chopped chives.

Savoury cream
Whip cream until fairly stiff. Add a few drops of lemon juice, seasoning, and a little finely chopped chives.

Cream cheese
Blend soft cream cheese with a little milk or cream, chopped parsley and chives.

Cottage cheese
Blend cottage cheese lightly with chopped nuts or chopped pineapple or chopped dates.

Cocktail Savouries and Snacks

The savouries for a cocktail party can be varied—and served either hot or cold. There is, however, one thing they should have in common—they must be small enough for people to pick up and eat without needing a plate. Ideally they should be small enough to be eaten in one mouthful.

If serving hot savouries they must be well drained so they do not make peoples' fingers greasy or sticky.

For a well planned cocktail party menu have
1 some savouries with cheese (see pages 50–51)
2 something with fish (see page 51)
3 something with bacon and/or other meat (see page 53)
4 something hot—although this is not essential (see page 51)
5 low-calorie 'titbits', for people watching their weight, such as radishes, gherkins, onions
6 salted nuts, crisps, etc.

Base for cocktail savouries
In order to balance the small pieces of food easily you need a base and this can be made from

Toast
This has the disadvantage of becoming 'soggy' in a relatively short time, but it is generally used for the basis of aspic savouries.

Fresh bread and butter
This is ideal for tiny pieces of smoked salmon, herring, etc.

Biscuits

Use either cheese biscuits or some of the great variety of cocktail-size biscuits available today.

Fried bread

Excellent since it can be prepared earlier in the day and either reheated for hot savouries or drained well and kept ready for cold savouries —it does not become soft for some hours.

Pancakes

Use the recipe for Scotch pancakes (see page 81) and make them the size of a half-penny; this makes very good base for rather soft pâté, which will make even fried bread soften in a short time.

Choux pastry

Use this as a filling case (see page 48).

Pastry

As well as making miniature pastry cases (see savoury horns, page 86), you can make penny-sized tartlet cases to be filled, or just roll out the pastry and cut into rounds about the size of a halfpenny or penny, bake and use as the base for savouries; or make vols au vent (see page 83).

Canapés or small savouries

The quickest way to make savouries, particularly if serving on bread, toast or fried bread, is to cut large slices, butter them, then cover the whole slice with the topping. Cut into bite-size pieces and garnish each piece. Try to arrange ingredients, etc. in order of working; this is not only quicker, but more efficient. Cover the cocktail savouries with foil or polythene to keep them fresh and moist.

To make aspic savouries or canapés

Aspic canapés look most attractive, and the aspic jelly topping is practical, since it ensures that the food below is kept moist.

you will need:

aspic jelly
base (either toast, biscuits, bread)
topping—this can be:
● eggs—hard-boiled, sliced or firmly scrambled

● fish—sardines, smoked or fresh-cooked salmon, sild pieces of herring
● meat—pâté, tongue, ham, salami
● vegetables—asparagus tips, tiny shapes or cooked carrot, beetroot, peas, beans

1 Make the aspic jelly according to packet directions, and allow to become lightly set but still soft enough to spread or brush over the food.
2 Arrange the food on long slices of the chosen base to give good colour and flavour contrast.
3 Lift the slices on to flat, clean trays or pastry board, so that any surplus jelly can be picked up and used again.
4 Either spread the jelly over the food with a warm palette knife or brush over, using a dry pastry brush; if using a pastry brush, do this several times to give a good layer.
5 Some of the jelly will drip down the sides—pick this up and use again.
6 For perfect results you may find it best to allow the jelly to set then brush over with a liquid layer of cold jelly to give a final smooth result.
7 Allow to set firmly, then cut into desired shapes with a sharp knife dipped in hot water.

Uncooked cheese savouries

By using different kinds of cheese you can provide a considerable variety of cocktail savouries with the minimum of preparation.

With fruit

Choose a fairly firm cheese that can be cut into small dice without crumbling. Put on cocktail sticks with:
● cubes or balls of melon (cut the balls with a vegetable scoop)
● ripe green or black grapes
● segments of well drained canned mandarins, or diced canned or fresh pineapple
● slices of banana—sprinkled with lemon juice to keep the colour
● firm Cheddar, Derby, Double Gloucester, Wensleydale, Dutch or processed cheese—all blend excellently with fruit

With ham

● Arrange small cubes of ham on buttered

biscuits and top with a teaspoon or piped rosette of cream cheese and a dusting of paprika.

● Put cubes of ham and of a fairly sharp cheese—Lancashire, Leicester—on to cocktail sticks with small onions.

With fish
● Use the same kinds of cheese as for fruit and put on to cocktail sticks with prawns or shrimps.
● Arrange tiny cubes or slices of cheese on buttered biscuits and top with rolled anchovy fillets.

With vegetables
● Blend either Danish blue, Stilton, cream cheese, grated Cheddar or other firm cheeses, with a little butter or mayonnaise and use as a filling for the centre of celery stalks—or the base of chicory.
Cut into $\frac{1}{2}$–1 inch lengths and top with chopped parsley and/or a dusting of paprika.
If the mixture is very soft and smooth it can be piped on to the pieces of celery.
● Grate equal quantities of cheese—or use soft cream cheese—and young carrots. Blend well; if using a firm cheese add a small amount of butter to give a consistency you can roll into balls. Make the balls about the size of a hazel nut and roll in chopped parsley or chopped nuts—various seasonings can be added as wished.
● Put cubes of cheese on cocktail sticks with tiny gherkins or halves of gherkin and cocktail onions.

With nuts
● Sandwich walnut halves with soft cream cheese or grated cheese blended with a little butter or margarine.
● Mix soft cream cheese with chopped salted peanuts and roll in balls.

Cooked cheese savouries

Since cheese toughens with over-cooking, timing of the savouries is important. If you have no help in the kitchen, put the savouries on to oven proof dishes, heat or brown as required, and serve on the same dish.

With bacon or sausage
● Wrap tiny cubes or fingers of cheese in small pieces of bacon, secure with wooden cocktail sticks and cook in the oven until the bacon is crisp.
● Insert a thin finger of cheese into tiny cooked cocktail or Frankfurter sausages and heat in the oven for a few minutes until the cheese melts.

As toasted snacks
● Make Welsh rarebit recipes (see page 45), brown under the grill or in the oven and cut into tiny cubes before serving.
● Or put the Welsh rarebit mixture on to fried bread or pancakes and heat for a few minutes.

Fried
● Coat cubes of cheese with egg and crumbs and fry for a few minutes until crisp and golden brown.
● Make very tiny Cheese fritters (see page 80), or Cheese meringues (see page 79).

Savouries with fish

Some of the tinned fish make a most suitable cocktail savoury—anchovies, herring titbits, pieces of rollmop herring, sardines, for example. Or try the following:

Smoked fish, eel, trout, kipper, salmon.
Shellfish, crab, lobster, prawns, shrimps.
Fresh cooked fish, white fish, salmon.
Fish roes, caviare, cod's roe.

Anchovies
● Chop the fillets and blend with chopped hard-boiled egg and enough butter or mayonnaise to make a thick paste. Pile on to rounds of buttered bread or biscuits. Garnish with capers or parsley.
● Twist fillets of anchovy round stuffed olives and arrange on buttered biscuits or flat dishes.
● Make miniature portions of Scotch Woodcock (see page 47).
● Use tiny pieces for aspic canapés.

Herring titbits

- Arrange on a bed of lettuce and put a pile of cocktail sticks beside the dish.
- Put on brown bread and butter with little watercress.
- Garnish with little butter flavoured with mustard and piped into small stars; serve either on bread (with no butter) or crisp bread.

Rollmop herring

Can be served as herring titbits and on cocktail sticks with tiny cocktail onions.

Sardines

- Mash and pipe on top of rings of hard-boiled egg on rounds of buttered bread or biscuits.
- Serve miniature portions of Breton fingers (see page 47).
- Mash, season well with pepper and a little lemon juice, and pile into centre of celery sticks.
- Serve very tiny pieces of hot sardine on buttered toast.

Eel

- Remove the dark skin, cut into tiny pieces and serve on buttered brown bread garnished with scrambled egg or horseradish cream.
- Put tiny pieces on top of bread covered with watercress butter (see page 55).

Trout

- Flake the flesh from the skin and bones and mix with little horseradish cream; serve on toast.
- Put tiny pieces on buttered brown bread and garnish with horseradish sauce (see page 90) and watercress.

Kipper

- Flake pieces of cooked kipper and mix with hard-boiled egg and chopped watercress. If necessary blend with little oil and vinegar and season well. Put on buttered bread.
- Blend the flaked kipper flesh with finely diced cocktail onions and gherkins and spread on fingers of bread and butter.

Salmon

- Wrap pieces of smoked salmon round asparagus tips and cut into about ½-inch pieces.
- Put salmon on slices of buttered bread and garnish with horseradish sauce (see page 90) and watercress.
- Blend with scrambled egg, put on top of crisp toast or fried bread and garnish with parsley and a dusting of paprika.

Crab or lobster

- Flake flesh, blend with mayonnaise (see page 36) and little lemon juice and spread on buttered bread or biscuits.
- Blend with a little tomato purée and finely diced cucumber. Season well and pile on fingers of pastry or bread and butter; garnish with lemon.
- Choose hen lobster and blend the red roe (coral) with butter and seasoning. Spread on bread and top with lobster meat.

Prawns or shrimps

- Put on buttered bread and garnish with mayonnaise and watercress.
- Coat with beaten egg and crumbs, fry for a few minutes in hot fat, drain and serve on cocktail sticks. Serve with a dish of tartare sauce as a dip (see page 91).
- Arrange fresh shrimps or prawns on lettuce and serve with cocktail sticks and a dip of tomato flavoured mayonnaise (for this blend either a sieved tomato to each ¼ pint mayonnaise [see page 36] or use 1 tablespoon tomato ketchup or purée. Season with Tabasco, soy or Worcestershire sauce).
- Use under aspic jelly as canapés.

Cooked white fish or salmon or tuna.

- Blend equal quantities of cooked fish and creamy mashed potato together, bind with egg yolk and season well. Form into fish cakes the size of a penny, coat in egg white and crumbs and bake or fry until crisp. Stick cocktail sticks through them and serve while hot.
- Blend fish with little mayonnaise (see page 36) and chopped egg white. Form into pyramid shapes on buttered biscuits or rounds of bread and garnish with chopped or sieved egg yolk and parsley.
- Choose the tiniest tomatoes available. Halve, remove the centre flesh and chop this with flaked fish, gherkin and onion. Blend with thick mayonnaise (see page 36) and return to cases. Garnish with capers or gherkins.

Caviare

● Cover slices of brown bread and butter with a ring of hard-boiled egg and top with 1 teaspoon caviare.

● Hard-boil eggs, halve, remove the yolks and blend this with caviare. Pile back into white cases and cut each half through centre.

Cod's roe

● When smoked, blend with little butter and cayenne pepper and put on watercress butter (see page 55) spread on fingers of bread.

● When fresh add mayonnaise (see page 36) and seasoning and use as a filling for pieces of celery, or bind with egg yolks.

● Cut into small cubes and wrap in pieces of bacon rashers. Secure with wooden cocktail sticks and heat in the oven until bacon is crisp.

Mussel titbits

cooking time   8 minutes

you will need:

1–1½ pints mussels	small quantity of finely
18 small rounds of toast,	chopped watercress
or biscuits	few drops lemon juice
2 oz. margarine or	anchovy paste
butter	paprika

1 Put the mussels into a large saucepan, adding just enough water to cover bottom of pan.
2 Heat gently until mussels open.
3 Remove them from shells, discarding beards.
4 Spread toast or biscuit with mixture made by creaming margarine or butter and adding finely chopped watercress and lemon juice.
5 Put a mussel on each round, then pipe a ring of anchovy paste round it. Dust with paprika.

Haddock pyramids

no cooking

you will need for 24 savouries:

24 small rounds toast, or biscuits	1 tablespoon mayonnaise (see page 36)
4 oz. cooked haddock	sieved white of 1 hard-boiled egg
seasoning	gherkins or stuffed olives

1 Mince or flake the fish very finely, mixing with the mayonnaise and egg white.
2 Season well, then form into a pyramid and decorate with a ring of gherkin or olive.

Variation:

Lobster pyramids
Substitute flaked lobster for haddock.

Anchovy fingers

cooking time   10 minutes

you will need for 12–18 savouries:

4 oz. short crust pastry (see page 82)	egg or milk to brush pastry
1 tin anchovies	

1 Roll the pastry into a neat oblong shape and cut into 6 strips about 1½ inches wide.
2 Arrange anchovies along these strips, then fold as though making sausage rolls.
3 Cut into lengths of about 2–3 inches.
4 Put on to a baking tin, brushing the pastry with milk or egg.
5 Bake for a good 10 minutes just above the middle of a hot oven (450°F.—Gas Mark 7).
6 Serve plain or, when the fingers are cold, twist another fillet of anchovy in a spiral round the outside.

Anchovy and egg canapés

no cooking

you will need:

24 cocktail biscuits	3 hard-boiled eggs
little butter or mayonnaise (see page 36)	1 can rolled anchovy fillets

1 Cover the biscuits with butter or thick mayonnaise.
2 Cut the eggs into thin slices.
3 Put on the buttered biscuits and top with anchovy fillets—the neat roll fits well into the centre of the egg yolk.

Savouries with meat

The most useful meats to buy for cocktail savouries are salami, liver sausage or pâté, sausages or sausage meat, tongue and ham.

Salami

● Cut into tiny strips and arrange on fingers of bread and butter with scrambled egg.

● Roll strips round cocktail onions and secure with cocktail sticks.

● Chop salami and blend with chopped hard-boiled egg, mayonnaise (see page 36) and chopped parsley. Spread on toast, fingers of bread and butter, or biscuits.

Liver sausage or pâté

● If using liver sausage, blend with a little butter to give the consistency of pâté. Spread on buttered bread or tiny Scotch pancakes (see page 81) and top with capers or slices of gherkin.

● Remove stones from soaked cooked prunes and fill with liver pâté. Put on to cocktail sticks.

● Fill centre of celery sticks with liver pâté and cut into $\frac{1}{2}$-inch lengths.

Sausages

● Tiny cocktail sausages can be grilled, fried or baked until crisp and golden brown. Put on to cocktail sticks and serve hot or cold. To make them more interesting put one of these savoury dips in the centre:

Blend equal quantities of mayonnaise (see page 36) and ketchup together and flavour with little made mustard.

Make a white sauce and flavour with tomato ketchup and mustard.

● Cut cooked sausages into small pieces and put on cocktail sticks with pieces of pineapple and gherkin.

● Blend sausage meat with little finely chopped cocktail onion and gherkin. Form into balls about the size of a hazel nut. Roll in egg and breadcrumbs and cheese mixed, or chopped nuts, and bake in the oven for about 10 minutes until crisp and brown and cooked.

Tongue and ham

● Cut tiny strips and roll into a cornet shape round soft cream cheese or cream cheese mixed with chopped gherkins, capers and parsley.

● Dice ham and put on cocktail sticks with pieces of fresh or canned pineapple or melon.

● Roll strips of tongue round tiny pieces of mustard pickle. Secure with cocktail sticks.

Bacon

● Roll small pieces of bacon round pieces of seasoned chicken liver. Secure with a cocktail stick and cook in a hot oven until the bacon is crisp.

● Make miniature portions of Devils on horseback or Angels on horseback (see page 46).

● Roll small pieces of bacon round cocktail-size cooked sausages or Frankfurter sausages—which have been split and filled with chutney or mustard pickle. Secure with cocktail sticks and cook until crisp and brown.

● Fry bacon rinds very slowly, until they are as crisp as possible. Cut or break into small lengths, toss in Parmesan cheese and serve little dishes of these instead of potato crisps.

Quick cocktail snacks with vegetables

Vegetables not only give colour but can provide a good variety of quick cocktail savouries.

Asparagus

● Lay cooked or well drained asparagus tips on slices of fresh brown bread and butter then roll firmly and cut into $\frac{1}{2}$–1 inch lengths. The bread must be fresh and have the crusts removed.

● Arrange tiny tips on scrambled egg or chopped hard-boiled egg blended with mayonnaise (see page 36).

Beetroot

● Use as the basis of aspic canapés.

● Tiny pieces of beetroot can be used as garnish on cheese savouries or on small pieces of herring on biscuits or bread and butter.

Corn on the cob

● The cooked corn can be blended with cream cheese and Parmesan cheese as a filling for tiny pastry cases.

● Corn is delicious blended with ham butter (see page 55) as a topping for bread and butter.

Carrots

● Thin strips of carrot or tiny washed carrots can be served either by themselves or round a dish of cream cheese dip (see page 55).

For Cream cheese dip: blend 8 oz. soft cream cheese with 2 tablespoons cream, seasoning, and a little chopped gherkin and onion, put into small dish.

Celery
● Pieces of celery can be filled with soft cheese mixtures, or with ham, or with fish blended with mayonnaise or liver pâté (see pages 36, 41).
● Use celery curls as garnish for many savouries—very thin long strips of celery, put into very cold water for a few hours, will curl tightly. Dry well before serving.

Mushrooms
● Tiny cooked mushrooms can be reheated on crisp fried bread—do this on the serving plate.
Stuffed mushrooms can be made to look most attractive. Cook and allow mushrooms to cool. Carefully remove the stalks and pipe rosettes of cream cheese, or put cheese or ham butter (see this page), or scrambled egg in the centres. Lift on to biscuits, rounds of toast or buttered bread. Garnish with paprika or chopped parsley and put stalks back in position.
● Neat slices of lightly cooked or raw mushrooms can be used on aspic canapés.

Tomatoes
● Halve tiny tomatoes and mix the centre pulp with cream cheese and diced gherkin. Pile back into tomato cases and top with a rose shape of cream cheese.

● Halve tiny tomatoes and mix centre pulp with mayonnaise (see page 36) and chopped prawns. Pile into cases and garnish with prawns.
● Halve tiny tomatoes and mix centre pulp with minced meat or chicken. Season well and blend with beaten egg. Heat for about 5–8 minutes in the oven so tomatoes and filling are hot but tomato cases are unbroken. Serve at once.

Flavoured butters

The flavour of toasted snacks can be made much more interesting by mixing the butter with any of the following:

Anchovy Add a little anchovy essence or few chopped anchovies.

Cheese Allow 1–2 oz. finely grated cheese to the same amount of butter. Add a little mustard and seasoning.

Curry Add $\frac{1}{2}$–1 teaspoon curry powder or curry paste to each ounce of butter.

Ham Add 1–2 oz. finely chopped ham to each ounce of butter.

Lobster Blend the red coral (roe of a hen lobster) to 2 oz. butter.

Parsley Add 1–2 teaspoons chopped parsley to each oz. butter with a little lemon juice.

Watercress Add 1–2 tablespoons finely chopped watercress to each oz. butter, season and add little lemon juice.

Savouries for Suppers and Light Meals

In the following pages are a selection of savouries that can be served as light meals. Some of them can be used as hors-d'œuvre, if a smaller portion is prepared.

Egg dishes

There is probably no more versatile food than an egg, which can be combined with other ingredients, or can make the basis of a good savoury by itself.
Whatever method you choose, do not overcook, for both flavour and texture are easily spoiled.

Baked eggs

cooking time   10–12 minutes

you will need for 4 servings:

1 oz. butter	seasoning
4 eggs	2 tablespoons cream

1 Grease 4 individual baking dishes with butter.
2 Break an egg into each, season well and cover with cream.
3 Bake slowly for about 10–12 minutes in a very moderate oven (350°F.—Gas Mark 3) until the eggs are just set.
4 Alternatively, steam in a pan of hot water.

Boiled eggs

cooking time   3½–10 minutes

you will need:

eggs   water

1 Put sufficient water into a saucepan to cover the eggs.
2 Bring the water to the boil, then lower the eggs gently into it.
3 Time carefully, and boil either 3½–4 minutes if you require a soft egg, 7–10 minutes for a firm egg.

10 ways of using boiled eggs

● Put hard-boiled eggs into cold water for 1 minute, then remove the shells. Coat with cheese sauce (see page 89) and grated cheese and brown under the grill.

● Follow instructions above, but put the eggs on a bed of cooked, sieved spinach.

● Shell soft-boiled eggs carefully by putting immediately into cold water for 1 minute, very gently tapping the shell and peeling. Coat with cheese sauce (see page 89) and put under the grill for just 1 minute.

● Shell the soft-boiled eggs as described above, coat with mushroom sauce, a layer of crumbs, and a little margarine; brown under the grill.

● Put layers of sliced hard-boiled egg and cooked sprigs of cauliflower into a shallow dish. Top with cheese sauce (see page 89) and brown under the grill.

● Make a quick tomato sauce (see page 91), put the shelled hard-boiled eggs in this and heat for just 1 minute. Serve on top of cooked rice.

● Halve hard-boiled eggs, remove yolks and mash them with a little butter, curry powder and chutney. Pipe or pile back again into white cases and serve on bed of lettuce.

● Halve hard-boiled eggs, remove yolk, mash with sardine, seasoning and a little lemon juice. Pile back again into white cases and serve on bed of lettuce.

● Hard-boiled eggs can also be served on spinach with a cheese sauce (see page 89).

● Shell hard-boiled eggs and arrange on crisp rounds of fried bread. Brush with a little melted butter, spread with a smooth chutney blended with a little curry powder. Sprinkle with crumbs, and put for 1 minute under a hot grill.

Egg and banana curry

cooking time   1 hour

you will need for 4 servings:

For the sauce:	
1 onion, chopped	1 dessertspoon
1 clove garlic, finely	redcurrant jelly
chopped	juice ½ lemon
1 tablespoon oil or 1 oz.	1 oz. sultanas
fat	
2 dessertspoons curry	4 bananas
powder	1 dessertspoon oil or
1 teaspoon curry paste	½ oz. fat
1 oz. cornflour	squeeze lemon juice
1 chicken stock cube	6–8 oz. long grain rice
¾ pint water	
1 apple, finely chopped	**To garnish:**
	3 eggs, hard-boiled
	watercress

1 Fry the onion and garlic in the heated oil.
2 Stir in the curry powder, curry paste, cornflour and crumbled stock cube.
3 Cook for 3–4 minutes.
4 Add water, apple, jelly, lemon juice and sultanas.
5 Bring to the boil, stirring, and simmer gently for 1 hour.
6 Place the bananas loosened from but still in their skins in an ovenproof dish.
7 Brush each banana with the oil and sprinkle with lemon juice.
8 Bake for about 15 minutes in a moderate oven (375°F.—Gas Mark 4).
9 While the curry is cooking, boil the long grain rice by one of the methods given on page 70. Arrange on a hot dish with the curry on top, garnish with the hard-boiled eggs and watercress and serve the baked bananas separately.

Fried eggs

cooking time   few minutes

you will need:

fat   eggs

1 Heat a little fat in the frying pan.
2 Break eggs into a saucer and slide into pan. Tilt the pan slightly as each egg goes in to keep the white a good shape.
3 If you like a crisp skin at the bottom of the eggs, turn the heat very low so that you get this without over-cooking the yolk.
4 If you like the top of the yolk covered with white, spoon a little fat over the yolk as it cooks.

10 ways to serve fried egg

1 The favourite and obvious way is *with bacon,* frying the bacon in the pan first, pushing to one side so that the eggs are actually fried in the bacon fat.

2 *On fried potato cakes*—make these by mashing potato with a little parsley, margarine, and seasoning, forming into cakes. Coat with flour, fry in pan until crisp and brown on either side. Top with a fried egg.

3 *On savoury fried rice*—fry a chopped onion in a little fat together with 2 chopped, skinned tomatoes, add 3 oz. cooked rice and seasoning. When hot, put into serving dish. Top with fried eggs.

4 *In a nest*—cut a circle in the centre of a slice of bread; fry one side until crisp and golden brown. Turn, carefully pour the egg into the centre hole, then fry the eggs and the second side of bread together.

5 *On sausage cakes*—form sausage meat into tiny cakes, adding mixed herbs if wished, then fry until crisp and golden brown, and top with fried eggs.

6 *Top cooked spaghetti* with fried eggs.

7 *Top baked beans* with fried eggs.

8 *Top fish cakes* with fried eggs.

9 *Top slices of fried corned beef* or luncheon meat with fried eggs.

10 *Tomato fried eggs*—fry tomatoes until just soft in pan, break eggs on to hot purée and fry gently until the white and yolk are just set.

Omelettes and fillings

For a substantial omelette allow 2 eggs per person; if making omelettes for a number of people do not try to cook too many eggs at a time—it is better to use a maximum of 4–6 (enough for an omelette for 2–3 people) in a 7–8 inch pan. If you cook a larger number the process is too slow and the eggs tend to toughen.

For a plain (or French) omelette, whisk the eggs lightly with seasoning, adding a little water if wished (allowing about 1 dessertspoon to each egg).

Heat a good knob of butter or spoonful of oil in the omelette pan, put in the eggs and allow to set lightly on the bottom, then work the mixture by loosening the omelette from the sides of the pan and tilt so that the liquid flows underneath. Put in the filling, fold or roll away from the handle and tip on to a hot dish.

For a soufflé omelette the whites and yolks are separated and the stiffly beaten whites folded into the beaten egg yolk. This tends to give a drier but of course thicker and lighter omelette and can be set more satisfactorily if given a minute or so cooking in the usual way and then set under a moderately hot grill, or finished cooking in the oven if the handle of the pan permits.

Adding filling to an omelette

There are two ways of doing this:

1 Cook the filling (i.e. bacon and tomato, or mixed vegetables, or fish) in a separate pan, add this to the eggs before folding the omelette.

2 The mixture can be cooked in the omelette pan in extra butter or oil. This has the advantage that you allow the eggs to absorb all the interesting flavour and use one pan only, but the omelette may stick and it is not easy to keep the omelette pan immaculate.

10 omelette fillings without cooking

1 *Anchovy* Add approximately 2 chopped anchovies per person to the beaten eggs. Be sparing with the salt. When the omelette has been folded, garnish with a lattice of anchovy fillets.

2 *Cheese* Allow 1–2 oz. grated cheese per person. Either mix with the beaten eggs (TAKE CARE THE OMELETTE IS NOT OVERCOOKED, OR IT WILL BECOME VERY TOUGH) or put the cheese in before folding.

3 *Beetroot* Allow approximately 1 tablespoon grated cooked beetroot per person. Put on top of the eggs when half set.

4 *Cream cheese* Put spoonfuls of cream cheese on to the half-set eggs and continue cooking.

5 *Cottage cheese* Put spoonfuls of cottage cheese on to the half-set eggs and continue cooking.

6 *Herb* Allow a good $\frac{1}{4}$ teaspoon dried herbs or 1–1$\frac{1}{2}$ teaspoons chopped fresh herbs per person. Add to the eggs when beaten.

7 *Prawns* Allow approximately 1–2 oz. finely chopped prawns per person. Add to the eggs when beating.

8 *Shrimps* Allow approximately 1–2 oz. finely chopped shrimps per person. Add to the eggs when beating.

9 *Smoked salmon* Allow $\frac{1}{2}$–1 oz. smoked salmon per person. Add to the eggs when beating.

10 *Parsley* Allow 1–2 teaspoons chopped parsley per person and add to the eggs when beating.

10 luxury ways to serve an omelette

These are equally suitable for an hors-d'œuvre or a main dish:

1 *Asparagus* Fill the omelette with cooked fresh or canned asparagus tips and garnish with asparagus.

2 *Brandy omelette* Add a little brandy to the beaten eggs and serve the omelette sprinkled with a little warm brandy. This is particularly delicious if you also fill with chopped hot prawns or shrimps.

3 *Caviare* Put either black or red caviare into the omelette just before serving.

4 *Ham* Toss diced York ham and red peppers or smoked Parma ham in a little hot butter. Put into the omelette just before serving.

5 *Liver pâté* Put liver pâté into the omelette just before serving. Garnish with lemon.

6 *Mushrooms* Either add chopped fried mushrooms to the beaten eggs before cooking, or fill with mushrooms or a really creamy mushroom sauce.

7 *Prawns* Either toss the prawns in hot butter and a little brandy, or sherry, or heat in a really creamy sauce. Put into the omelette before folding.

8 *Smoked salmon* Add strips of smoked salmon to the omelette just before it is set.

9 *Omelette provençale* Fry diced aubergines, diced red peppers and/or green peppers and tomatoes in a little hot butter. Put into the omelette just before folding.

10 *Savoury cream* Beat a little Parmesan cheese into whipped cream, together with seasoning and finely chopped fresh herbs. Put into the omelette just before serving.

10 ways to make an omelette go further

1 *Bread* Allow approximately ½ slice of bread per person. Cut into small dice. Fry until crisp and golden brown in extra hot butter or oil. Pour the eggs over the crisp bread and cook in the usual way.

2 *Beans* Allow approximately 1 tablespoon cooked haricot or baked beans per person. Heat in a little hot butter or oil. Pour the eggs over the beans and cook in the usual way.

3 *Bacon* Use cheap pieces of bacon. Dice and fry in pan. Add the butter or oil. Heat and make the omelette in the usual way.

4 *Potato* Allow 1 sliced cooked potato per person. Fry in extra hot butter or oil. Pour the eggs over the crisp potatoes and cook in the usual way.

5 *Lyonnaise* Allow ½ onion, sliced, and 1 cooked potato per person. Fry steadily in hot oil or butter until the onion is transparent and tender. Add extra butter or oil if necessary. Pour on the eggs and cook in the usual way.

6 *Tomato* Allow 1–2 tomatoes per person. Cook tomatoes separately as they are inclined to make the omelette sticky. Add to the half-set omelette or to the beaten eggs and cook in the usual way.

7 *Mixed vegetable* Allow 1–2 tablespoons mixed cooked vegetables per person. Either heat in hot butter or oil in the omelette pan or heat separately. Add to beaten eggs or pour eggs over the hot vegetables. Cook in the usual way.

8 *Medley omelette* Fry a small quantity of diced cooked potato, onion, bacon and tomato. When soft, either put in the centre of egg mixture, or add to the beaten eggs.

9 *Add cornflour* Blend 2 teaspoons cornflour with a little milk or water and beat eggs into it.

10 Add a little *cooked pasta* or *cooked rice*.

Scrambled eggs

To scramble eggs

cooking time · few minutes

you will need:

butter or margarine	seasoning
eggs	a little milk if desired*

*For a softer but less rich scrambled egg

1 Allow 1–2 eggs per person and up to 1 tablespoon milk.
2 Heat a good knob of butter or margarine in a saucepan, pour in the eggs beaten with the seasoning, and cook steadily, stirring well from the bottom until the mixture starts to thicken.
3 Turn the heat very low and continue cooking until set as firm as you like.

Note:
A very good way to cook scrambled egg with minimum waste and a very creamy consistency is in the top of a double saucepan or in a basin over hot water.

10 ways to make a scrambled egg savoury

1 *In bacon nests* Twist rashers of bacon into circles and grill or fry while scrambling the eggs. Put creamy scrambled egg in the centre and serve at once.

2 *With cheese* Add 1 oz. of grated cheese to each 1–2 eggs. Put in the cheese as the mixture starts to thicken.

3 *With ham* Heat finely diced ham in butter or margarine, then add eggs.

4 *With chicken* Heat finely diced cooked chicken in butter or margarine then add eggs and continue as for scrambled egg.

5 *With prawns or shrimps* Blend these with beaten eggs and cook gently in hot butter or margarine.

6 *With finnan haddock* Heat flaked fish in hot butter or margarine. Add beaten eggs and continue as scrambled egg.

7 *With vegetables* Heat 1–2 tablespoons cooked vegetables per person in hot butter or margarine. Add eggs and continue as for scrambled eggs.

8 *With crisp crumbs* Use rather more butter or margarine than usual and fry about 1 tablespoon crumbs per person in this until they are crisp and golden but not too brown. Add the eggs and continue as for scrambled eggs.

9 *With potato* Use rather more butter or margarine than usual and toss 1 diced potato in this for each person. Add scrambled eggs with a little chopped chives or parsley and cook in the usual way.

10 *With mixed vegetables* Allow 1 skinned tomato, 1 teaspoon chopped onion, a little chopped red or green pepper per person. Do not use milk with the egg. Put in rather more butter or margarine than usual. Toss the vegetables in this then add beaten and seasoned eggs and scramble in the usual way.

How to use poached eggs

To poach an egg

cooking time   3 minutes

you will need:

eggs   seasoning
butter

1 If using a poacher, put a piece of butter into each cup and allow to melt.
2 Carefully slide an egg into the cup and season.
3 Put the lid on the pan and allow the water to boil steadily for about $3\frac{1}{2}$–4 minutes.
4 Slide the egg on to buttered toast.
5 If not using a poacher, bring a good $\frac{1}{2}$ pint water to boil in a saucepan or frying pan.
6 Add 1 dessertspoon vinegar to prevent the egg whites spreading.
7 Add salt and slide the eggs into the boiling water.
8 Leave for 3 minutes, or until egg whites are set.
9 Carefully remove eggs with fish slice and put on toast.

10 ways with poached egg supper snacks

1 *Poached eggs Florentine* Put the poached eggs on to a bed of cooked spinach.

2 *Poached eggs mornay* Put the poached eggs on to buttered toast, coat with cheese sauce (see page 89) and brown for 1 minute under a hot grill.

3 *Poached egg au gratin* Put the poached eggs on to hot buttered toast, top with a good layer of breadcrumbs and grated cheese, then brown for 1 minute under the grill.

4 *Savoury poached eggs* Make a ratatouille (see page 76) and add just a little extra liquid. Cook the ratatouille mixture in a rather wide pan or deep frying pan. Drop the eggs into this and allow to set, or poach separately and serve on top of each portion of mixed vegetables.

5 *Poached eggs in wine* Heat cheap red wine in a shallow pan and poach the eggs in this.

6 *Poached eggs on gammon* Grill slices of gammon, top with grilled tomatoes and poached eggs.

7 *Poached eggs on haddock* Cook portions of finnan haddock in water or milk and top each with a poached egg.

8 *Tomato poached eggs* Put either tomato juice, tomato soup or tomato purée into a wide pan or deep frying pan. Break the eggs into this and poach in the usual way. Serve with crisp toast or French bread.

9 *Poached egg in consommé* Although this is generally served as a soup, it can also be a light savoury. Make the consommé (see page 15), adding a little sherry, but cooking in either a wide saucepan or deep frying pan. Poach the eggs in this and serve in soup cups with French bread.

10 *Scotch pancakes topped with poached egg* Make Scotch pancakes (see page 81) and top with poached eggs.

Soufflés can be easy

A soufflé sounds extremely difficult but it is, in fact, very easy. Here are the rules to follow:

For a hot soufflé When adding the egg yolks make sure the sauce or other purée is sufficiently cool so the yolks will not curdle.

Fold the egg whites in very gently so you do not lose the fluffy texture.

Preparing dish for hot soufflé Providing the mixture only comes about two-thirds of the way up the dish before being cooked, there is no need for any special preparation. You can, however, put band of buttered paper to support the weight of the mixture as it rises, if the dish is to be filled very lavishly. It does, as a matter of fact, make a very attractive looking soufflé if it has risen high above the top.

Serving hot soufflés Time the cooking of a soufflé so it can be served the moment it comes out of the oven.

Cold soufflés When adding the egg whites in a cold soufflé, make absolutely certain that the jellied mixture is partially set so that it will hold the egg whites in position. If it is very runny, the egg whites float to the top and you will not have an even texture.

Preparing the dish for cold soufflés This should, of course, be done as suggested above, by putting a band of paper round the top (see Ham and mushroom soufflé, page 62).

Cheese and potato soufflé

cooking time	55 minutes

you will need:

1 lb. potatoes	seasoning
2–3 oz. grated cheese	2 eggs or
1 oz. margarine	1 egg and 1 teaspoon
2 tablespoons milk	baking powder
1 teaspoon finely	
chopped chives or	
grated onion	

1 Cook, drain and mash the potatoes well.
2 Beat in the margarine, milk, chives and cheese, then season well.
3 Stir in the well-beaten egg yolks and, when the mixture is cool, FOLD in the stiffly beaten egg whites and the baking powder, if this is being used.
4 Put into a well-greased soufflé dish and bake in the centre of a moderately hot oven (400°F.—Gas Mark 5) for 30 minutes until well risen and crisp and brown on top.

Corn cob soufflé

cooking time	45 minutes–1 hour

you will need for 4 servings:

2–3 corn cobs or	1 oz. margarine
frozen or canned corn	seasoning
on the cob	2–3 eggs
½ pint milk	4 oz. grated cheese
1 teaspoon flour	a little chopped parsley
1 teaspoon cornflour	or chives

1 Boil cobs until tender and scrape corn from the cobs.
2 Make the white sauce from the milk, flour, cornflour and margarine, season and remove from the heat.
3 Add the beaten egg yolks, 3 oz. of the cheese, chopped parsley or chives and corn.
4 Fold in the stiffly beaten whites of eggs.
5 Put into an ovenproof dish, sprinkle with the rest of the cheese, dot with margarine.
6 Bake in a very moderate oven (350°F.—Gas Mark 3) for 30–45 minutes until light brown.

Ham soufflé

cooking time	35–40 minutes

you will need:

4 oz. cooked ham	1 oz. grated cheese,
1 oz. butter or	optional
margarine	4 eggs or 3 yolks and
¾ oz. flour	4 whites
¼ pint milk	seasoning
	good pinch herbs

1 Chop the ham into small pieces, heat the butter then stir in the flour.
2 Cook for a few minutes then gradually add the milk.
3 Bring to the boil and cook until smooth and thick.
4 Add the grated cheese, ham, seasoning, herbs and egg yolks.
5 Whisk the egg whites until stiff.
6 Fold egg whites into the ham mixture.
7 Put into a prepared soufflé dish and bake for approximately 25–30 minutes in the centre of a moderately hot oven (400°F.—Gas Mark 5).

Note:

This soufflé is an excellent main dish, for the ham makes it filling as well as nourishing.

Salmon rice soufflé

cooking time   40 minutes

you will need for 4 servings:

1 oz. margarine	2 oz. long-grain rice,
1 oz. flour	cooked
$\frac{1}{4}$ pint milk	3 eggs
1 medium can pink	seasoning
salmon	

1 Make a sauce of the margarine, flour and milk.
2 Add can of salmon, the rice, then stir in the egg yolks and the stiffly beaten egg whites. Season.
3 Put into the prepared soufflé dish and bake for approximately 30 minutes in the centre of a moderate oven (375°F.—Gas Mark 4).

Spinach soufflé

cooking time   40–50 minutes

you will need for 4 servings:

8 oz. cooked spinach	pinch nutmeg
1$\frac{1}{2}$ oz. butter	5 tablespoons sieved
$\frac{1}{2}$ oz. flour	breadcrumbs
2$\frac{1}{2}$ tablespoons milk	6 eggs
salt and pepper	$\frac{1}{4}$ pint whipped cream

1 Drain the spinach as dry as possible and chop very finely.
2 Make a thick cream sauce of the butter, flour and milk.
3 Add seasonings and nutmeg and cool.
4 Add spinach and half the breadcrumbs and mix thoroughly.
5 Beat egg yolks lightly and the egg whites stiffly.
6 Add the yolks and cream to the spinach mixture, then fold in the egg whites.
7 Butter a soufflé dish and scatter with remaining crumbs.
8 Pour in the mixture which should fill two-thirds of the dish.
9 Bake for 30–45 minutes in a pan of hot water in a moderate oven (375°F.—Gas Mark 4).

Ham and mushroom soufflé

cooking time   15 minutes

you will need for 4 servings:

1 packet mushroom soup	1 tablespoon chopped
$\frac{1}{2}$ pint water	parsley
4 oz. finely chopped ham	2 tablespoons whipped
$\frac{1}{2}$ oz. powdered gelatine	cream
2 egg whites	seasoning
2 hard-boiled eggs	

1 Make up mushroom soup with only $\frac{1}{2}$ pint water.
2 Simmer as detailed on the packet.
3 Soften the gelatine in 1 tablespoon water then dissolve in the hot mushroom soup; cool and fold in cream, chopped ham, seasoning and the stiffly beaten egg whites.
4 Pour into 1 pint soufflé dish prepared with a band of buttered paper tied firmly round the outside, and which should stand up several inches above the top of the dish.
5 Leave until firm.
6 Remove paper.
7 Chop 1 hard-boiled egg and sprinkle this with the chopped parsley round edge of soufflé.
8 Cut remaining egg into 8 fingers and arrange in centre.

Light cheese snacks

Cheese is such an adaptable savoury in that it is particularly suitable for the end of a meal or for a cocktail party and you will find most of the cheese recipes in this section are equally suitable for a main dish savoury if served in rather larger quantities.

Cheese kabobs

cooking time   approximately 3 minutes

you will need:

Cheddar cheese	bacon
pieces of tomato	pickled onions
small squares of buttered	
bread	

1 Put cubes of cheese, pieces of tomato, buttered bread, bacon, and pickled onions alternately on to skewers.
2 Cover wire rack on grill pan with foil.
3 Place kabobs on foil and grill approximately 3 minutes, turning once.

Cheese and shellfish kabobs

cooking time   few minutes

you will need:

Cheddar cheese	butter
large prawns or shrimps	quarters of lemon

1 Put cubes of cheese, large prawns or shrimps, and quarters of lemon alternately on skewers.

2 Brush the prawns or shrimps with a little melted butter.

3 Cover wire rack on grill pan with foil.

4 Place kabobs on foil and grill approximately 3 minutes, turning once.

Fruit cheese kabobs

cooking time   approximately 3 minutes

you will need:

Cheddar cheese	banana
cubes dessert or fairly	pineapple
sweet apple	butter

1 Put cubes of cheese, apple, banana and pineapple alternately on to skewers.

2 Brush with a very little melted butter.

3 Cover wire rack on grill pan with foil.

4 Place kabobs on foil and grill for approximately 3 minutes, turning once.

Spanish cheese kabobs

cooking time   approximately 3 minutes

you will need:

Cheddar cheese	banana
pieces green pepper	tomato

1 Put cubes of cheese, pieces of green pepper, banana and tomato alternately on to skewers.

2 Cover wire rack on grill pan with foil.

3 Place kabobs on foil and grill approximately 3 minutes, turning once.

Cheese and prawn moulds

cooking time   few minutes

you will need for 4 servings:

½ pint aspic jelly	pinch pepper
6 oz. peeled prawns	¼ teaspoon salt
6 large radishes	few drops Tabasco
8 oz. grated Cheddar	sauce
cheese	3 tablespoons cream
½ lb. skinned tomatoes	

1 Pour enough aspic jelly into bottom of fish-shaped jelly mould (or 1¾-pint ring mould) to cover bottom thinly.

2 Allow to set.

3 Arrange some of the prawns in bottom of mould to represent scales of fish and place slices of radish for eyes, set in a little more aspic jelly.

4 Chop remaining radishes and prawns and add to cheese.

5 Remove seeds from tomatoes and chop pulp finely.

6 Stir into cheese mixture with salt and Tabasco sauce.

7 Fold in remaining aspic and cream.

8 Spoon into mould and allow to set, preferably chilling in refrigerator.

9 Warm mould slightly and turn out sharply on to serving dish.

10 Serve with crisp green salad.

Cheese charlotte

cooking time   few minutes

you will need for 4 servings:

2 oz. Cheddar cheese	2 oz. cream cheese
few slices thinly cut	½ teaspoon French
brown and white	mustard
bread and butter	pinch salt and cayenne
3 eggs	
2 teaspoons	**To garnish:**
powdered gelatine	almonds
3 tablespoons water	watercress
¼ pint cream or	
evaporated milk	

1 Grate Cheddar cheese.

2 Line a buttered charlotte mould or 5-inch cake tin with the bread, using alternate fingers of white and brown.

3 Whisk the egg yolks until thick and add the gelatine first soaked then dissolved in the very hot water.

4 Stir in the cream or evaporated milk, cheeses and seasonings, then fold in the stiffly whipped whites.

5 Turn the mixture into the charlotte mould and chill.

6 Turn out and serve garnished with watercress and decorated with almonds.

Fish and meat snacks

These will not be as substantial as a main dish, but pieces of left-over chicken, meat, or bacon can be used to make a very good savoury.

63

To cook cod's roe

cooking time   20 minutes

1 Wash the roe and steam or boil this for approximately 20 minutes.
2 Cut into slices and fry in a little fat until brown.
3 After steaming the roe, skin it, add seasoning, and spread on the slices of bread and butter.

Fried herring roes

cooking time   few minutes

you will need:

herring roes (fresh,   fat for frying
  canned or frozen)
flour   **To garnish:**
seasoning   parsley
                                paprika or cayenne

1 Allow the roes to defrost, then dry well on plenty of kitchen paper.
2 Roll in enough flour to coat thoroughly, seasoning this flour well.
3 Fry for a few minutes only in hot fat.
4 Garnish with parsley and paprika or cayenne; serve with vegetables or on hot buttered toast.

Fish sticks mornay

cooking time   approximately 10 minutes

you will need:

1 packet frozen fish   tomatoes
  sticks   fat for frying
little grated cheese

1 Separate the fish sticks and roll in grated cheese.
2 Halve the toamtoes.
3 Fry the cheese coated fish sticks, then the tomatoes in hot fat.*

*If preferred, these can be baked on a greased tin in the oven or brushed with melted fat after coating with cheese and cooked under a hot grill, turning over then coating with more cheese and melted fat

Bacon buntings

cooking time   4 minutes

you will need for 3 servings:

6 sausages, cooked   6 middle rashers bacon
1 tablespoon chutney

1 Split the cooked sausages and fill with chutney, pickle or mustard.
2 Trim the bacon rashers and stretch.

3 Wind each rasher spirally around the sausages and hold in place with a small wooden cocktail stick.
4 Put under the grill.
5 Cook and turn about four minutes.

Bacon and cheese

cooking time   few minutes

you will need:

rashers bacon   slices of cheese—
                                 preferably Cheddar

1 When frying bacon a slice of cheese is a very delicious accompaniment—add when the bacon is nearly cooked, and fry for a moment or so until the cheese starts to melt.
2 Then lift out and serve on top of the rashers of bacon.

Bacon medallions

cooking time   15–20 minutes

you will need for 4 servings:

4 thick middle rashers   4 tomatoes
  bacon   3 oz. cooked rice
3 oz. margarine or bacon
  fat   **To garnish:**
1 8-oz. can mushrooms   hard-boiled egg
1 red pepper   parsley
4 oz. runner beans   lemon

1 Remove rind from bacon and cut fat at $\frac{1}{2}$-inch intervals.
2 Put on grid of grill pan with halved tomatoes in the pan.
3 Brush with melted fat or margarine and cook under grill until tender and the fat golden brown.
4 Meanwhile, heat rest of fat in pan and cook mushrooms and thinly sliced red pepper until tender.
5 Add beans.
6 Saving a small amount of this mixture for garnish, bind rest with the cooked rice. Heat well and form into ring on hot dish.
7 Chop egg and parsley together.
8 Arrange slices of bacon and halved tomatoes in centre of rice ring.
9 Top one end of each bacon slice with slice lemon and the egg mixture and the other end with mushroom mixture, but leave centre clear as the pink of the bacon is so inviting.

Bacon and mushroom batter

cooking time   40 minutes

you will need for 4 servings:

4 oz. medium mushrooms	$\frac{1}{2}$ pint batter (see page 80)
1 oz. butter	seasoning
8 rashers lean bacon	

1 Put the mushrooms into an ovenproof dish, a dab of butter on each, and season well.
2 Roll the rashers, arrange in the dish and cook in a hot oven (450°F.—Gas Mark 7) for 10 minutes.
3 Pour in the batter and return to the oven for about 30 minutes.
4 Serve at once.

Hot bacon and oat cobbler

cooking time   30 minutes

you will need for 4 servings:

1 packet vegetable soup	2 oz. butter or margarine
scant 1 pint water	1 egg
3–4 rashers bacon (cut small and well fried)	milk (to make $\frac{1}{4}$ pint with egg)
6 oz. self-raising flour	little grated cheese
2 oz. rolled oats	
salt and pepper	

1 Cook the vegetable soup as instructed on the packet but using just under 1 pint of water.
2 Prepare bacon.
3 Sieve flour and seasonings into basin.
4 Add oats and mix thoroughly.
5 Rub butter in lightly.
6 Add bacon.
7 Beat egg and milk together and pour over dry ingredients, mixing with a broad-bladed knife.
8 Roll out on floured board to about $\frac{1}{2}$ inch thick and cut into rounds.
9 Put the vegetable soup into a casserole and heat for about 10 minutes in a moderately hot oven (400°F.—Gas Mark 5).
10 Arrange rounds of scone on top and sprinkle with grated cheese to give an attractive glaze.
11 Bake for approximately 12–15 minutes in a hot oven (450°F.—Gas Mark 7).

Bacon and pineapple loaf

cooking time   1 hour

you will need for 4 servings:

12 oz. bacon	1 15-oz. can pineapple slices
2 oz. fine breadcrumbs	
salt and pepper	**To garnish:**
pinch mixed herbs	watercress
1 egg	

1 Mince or chop bacon finely.
2 Add breadcrumbs, seasoning, a very small pinch of mixed herbs, the egg and about a tablespoon pineapple syrup from the can.
3 Blend well and put into a well-greased loaf tin.
4 Cover with greased paper and bake for approximately 1 hour in the centre of a moderate oven (375°F.—Gas Mark 4).
5 Turn out carefully and garnish with pineapple slices—replace for a few minutes in the oven to heat the pineapple then top with sprigs of watercress.

Peas with bacon

cooking time   20 minutes

you will need for 4 servings:

4 rashers bacon	$\frac{1}{2}$ teaspoon salt
2 lb. peas	

1 Dice bacon and fry in medium pan with tightly fitting lid over low heat until crisp.
2 Remove from heat and drain all but 1 tablespoon fat from the pan.
3 Add peas and remaining ingredients.
4 Cook, covered, over medium heat for 10–15 minutes, or until peas are just tender.

Savoury bacon dip

no cooking

you will need:

10 oz. cottage or cream cheese	1 tablespoon chopped parsley
8 oz. minced or chopped cooked bacon	$\frac{1}{4}$ teaspoon garlic salt
$\frac{1}{2}$ grated or minced onion	$\frac{1}{4}$ teaspoon pepper
	$\frac{1}{4}$ teaspoon salt

1 Sieve the cottage cheese or mash the cheese into a basin and add all the ingredients.
2 Blend well and allow to stand for about an hour.
3 Re-season to taste.
4 Serve with potato crisps, small biscuits or celery sticks.

Poultry snacks

Chicken cream

cooking time   15 minutes

you will need for 4 servings:

1 packet cream of chicken soup powder	1 lb. cooked chicken (as much breast as possible)
¾ pint milk	1–2 eggs
¼ oz. powdered gelatine	¼ pint evaporated milk
1 tablespoon water	1 tablespoon sherry
⅛ pint water or white stock	seasoning

1 Blend the soup with the milk and cook gently.
2 Dissolve the gelatine in the hot stock, first softening it in the tablespoon of water.
3 Mix together the soup and the gelatine liquid, allow this to cool and then add the chicken, beaten egg, evaporated milk and sherry.
4 Taste and season well.
5 Pour into rinsed mould or basin and allow to set.
6 Serve with plain green salad and fingers of toast.

Chicken flan

cooking time   50 minutes

you will need:

6–8 oz. flan or short-crust pastry (see page 82)	4 oz. coarsely grated Cheddar cheese
1 onion, chopped	2 tablespoons chopped parsley
1 small red or green pepper, finely chopped	salt and pepper
little fat	1 egg
6 oz. minced chicken	¼ pint milk

1 Prepare the flan case and bake it 'blind' (see page 84).
2 Toss the onion and pepper in a little hot fat.
3 Mix with the chicken, cheese and parsley.
4 Turn into the pastry case after thoroughly seasoning.
5 Beat the egg into the milk, season and pour into the flan case.
6 Bake in a moderate oven (375°F.—Gas Mark 4) for approximately 30 minutes.

Fricassée of chicken breasts

cooking time   45 minutes–1 hour

you will need for 4 servings:

4 frozen chicken breasts	1 oz. flour
1 oz. butter or margarine	¾ pint milk
	seasoning
	2 tablespoons cream

1 Allow chicken breasts to defrost at room temperature.
2 Make the sauce with the butter, flour and milk; season well.
3 Put in the chicken breasts and cook very slowly in a covered pan for approximately 35–45 minutes until tender.
4 Stir in the cream and re-season if wished.
5 Serve with cooked rice or crisp toast.

Variations:

Chicken and mushroom fricassée

As recipe above but use 2 oz. butter or margarine and fry 2–4 oz. chopped mushrooms before making the sauce—this gives a slightly darker mixture. If you prefer a lighter sauce, follow the above recipe, cooking the chicken breasts in the sauce, then fry the mushrooms SEPARATELY and stir into the sauce just before serving.

Golden chicken fricassée

Follow instructions for Fricassée of chicken breasts, but blend the yokes of 2 eggs or 2 whole eggs with the cream, add to the sauce and cook very gently WITHOUT BOILING for a few minutes.

Chicken à la King

cooking time   10–15 minutes

you will need for 4 servings:

1 sliced red pepper	seasoning
2 oz. mushrooms, sliced	1 tablespoon olives
2 oz. butter	4 slices toast
½ pint white sauce (see page 92) made partly with chicken stock	
12 oz. diced cooked chicken	**To garnish:** olives

1 Fry pepper and mushrooms in butter or cook under grill until soft.
2 Stir into sauce with other ingredients.
3 Pile on to toast.
4 Garnish with olives.

Chicken medley nest

cooking time   35 minutes

you will need for 4 servings:

1 lb. potatoes
knob butter
2 tablespoons milk
salt and pepper

For the filling:
2 tablespoons oil or
  2 oz. butter
1 onion, chopped

½ oz. cornflour or 1 oz.
  flour
½ pint milk
salt and pepper
8 oz. cooked chicken
4 oz. cooked ham
4 oz. sweet corn or
  cooked carrots
1 dessertspoon chopped
  parsley

1 Cook the potatoes in boiling salted water until tender.
2 Mash with butter, milk and seasoning to taste.
3 Pipe a thick border of creamed potato round the edge of a large fireproof dish. Brush with a little milk and brown under the grill.
4 To prepare the filling, heat the oil or butter and fry the onion until tender.
5 Add flour or cornflour and cook 1 minute.
6 Add milk, bring to the boil and cook 3 minutes, stirring all the time. Season to taste.
7 Add chicken, ham, sweet corn or carrots, and parsley and mix well.
8 Cook a further 3 minutes to heat through.
9 Pile into the potato shell and serve.

Turkey or chicken creole

cooking time   20 minutes

you will need for 4 servings:

4 oz. rice
1 oz. fat
1 green pepper, sliced
¼ pint turkey or chicken
  stock
1 head celery (or can
  celery)

about 12 oz. sliced
  cooked turkey or
  chicken meat
seasoning

To garnish:
3 large tomatoes, sliced

1 Cook rice in boiling salted water.
2 Heat fat and toss in it the sliced pepper and celery cut in large pieces.
3 Add stock.
4 Simmer until vegetables are nearly cooked.
5 Add turkey and season well.
6 When thoroughly hot, arrange on bed of the cooked rice.
7 Garnish with sliced tomato.

Snacks with meat
Baked corned beef with barbecue sauce

cooking time   30 minutes

you will need for 4 servings:

1 12-oz. can corned beef
a little dripping or
  margarine

For the sauce:
¼ pint boiling water
1 teaspoon curry powder
1 teaspoon Worcester-
  shire sauce

4 teaspoons tomato
  sauce
seasoning
1 teaspoon brown sugar
2 tablespoons tiny
  cocktail or pickling
  onions, optional

1 Grease a baking dish and put the corned beef into this, covering the top with greased paper.
2 Heat for about 15 minutes in a moderately hot oven (400°F.—Gas Mark 5), then remove the paper.
3 Meanwhile, blend all the ingredients for the sauce together.
4 Pour this over the corned beef and cook for a further 15 minutes, basting the meat several times with the sauce.

Corned beef scotch eggs

cooking time   15–20 minutes

you will need for 4 servings:

For the sauce:
1 oz. margarine
1 oz. flour
¼ pint milk or stock
3 oz. breadcrumbs

1 12-oz. can corned beef
seasoning
6 hard-boiled eggs
1 egg, beaten
fat for frying

1 To make the sauce, heat the margarine in the pan, stir in the flour and cook for 2 minutes, then add the liquid.
2 Bring to the boil and cook until thick.
3 Add most of the breadcrumbs and the flaked corned beef.
4 Season well.
5 Press the mixture round the outside of the shelled hard-boiled eggs.
6 When neatly shaped, brush with beaten egg, toss carefully in remaining breadcrumbs and fry until crisp and golden brown.

Hamburgers

cooking time   10–30 minutes

you will need for 4 servings:

1 lb. minced beef
1 large or 2 medium
  onions, grated
seasoning
$\frac{1}{2}$ teaspoon mixed herbs

1 heaped teaspoon
  chopped parsley
1 teaspoon Worcester-
  shire sauce
1 large potato

1 Put meat into a basin, add grated onion, seasoning, herbs, parsley and sauce.
2 Grate in raw peeled potato.
3 Mix thoroughly together. There will be no need to add liquid as the potato binds the mixture together.
4 Form into large cakes* and either fry steadily in hot fat for about 10 minutes or bake on a well greased tin for about 25–30 minutes in a moderately hot oven (400°F.—Gas Mark 5).
5 Serve hot and, if wished, with a fried egg on top.

*The cakes can be floured or tossed in crisp breadcrumbs before cooking—don't try to turn into a neat rissole shape

Hamburger 'hot pot'

cooking time   15 minutes

you will need:

1 large packet mixed
  frozen vegetables
1 can tomato soup
1 large packet frozen
  hamburgers

seasoning

To garnish:
chopped parsley
4 slices toast

1 Put the frozen vegetables into about $\frac{1}{4}$ inch salted water and cook for about 4 minutes.
2 Add the tomato soup and heat for a few minutes, stir briskly, then add the hamburgers, cook gently for about 8 minutes and season. If possible use a fairly large saucepan or even a frying pan, so that the hamburgers do not get broken in cooking.
3 Serve on a hot dish with a border of triangles of crisp toast, and topped with chopped parsley.

Hamburgers and sauce

cooking time   10 minutes

you will need for 4 servings:

8 oz. minced beef
1 chopped onion
2 oz. rolled oats
1 egg
2 oz. dripping or fat
salt and pepper

tomato sauce (see page
  91)

To garnish:
green pepper, cut in
  rings
tomatoes, cut in halves

1 Mix together the mince, onion, oats, egg and seasoning and divide into 4–8 round cakes.
2 Score the tops with the back of a knife.
3 Heat the dripping in a frying pan and cook the hamburgers for a few minutes on both sides.
4 Reduce the heat and cook gently for 5 minutes until they are cooked through.
5 Garnish with some gently fried pepper rings tomato halves and serve with tomato sauce.

Ham loaf de luxe

cooking time   35 minutes

you will need for 4 servings:

approximately 10 oz.
  cooked ham
2 teaspoons grated
  onion or chopped
  chives
2 teaspoons chopped
  parsley
1 can corn, or corn and
  peppers

1 egg to bind or thick
  sauce made from
  $\frac{1}{2}$ oz. flour $\frac{1}{2}$ oz.
  butter $\frac{1}{8}$ pint milk
1 tablespoon cream or
  top of milk
seasoning
2 hard-boiled eggs

1 Mince the ham with the onion, parsley, drained corn or corn and peppers, and the egg or sauce and cream.
2 Season lightly and press half the mixture into a greased loaf tin.
3 Arrange the 2 shelled eggs on top of this and cover with the rest of the mixture.
4 Put a piece of foil or greaseproof paper over the mixture and bake for approximately 35 minutes in the centre of a moderate oven (375°F.—Gas Mark 4).
5 Turn out and serve hot.

Savoury pruneburgers

cooking time   10 minutes

you will need for 4 servings:

seasoning
12 oz. minced beef
2 oz. butter or
  margarine
1 oz. flour
$\frac{1}{3}$ pint milk
1 tablespoon onions,
  finely chopped

2–3 cooked prunes,
  chopped
1–2 oz. almonds,
  toasted and slivered
8 fingers toast

To garnish:
8 prunes
parsley

1 Add seasoning to meat.
2 Melt butter in pan.
3 Add beef, cook for 2 minutes.

4 Push meat to one side.
5 Add flour to hot butter; stir until blended.
6 Add milk gradually, stirring constantly until sauce is thick and smooth.
7 Add onion and stir well.
8 Just before serving, stir in prunes and almonds.
9 Serve on hot toast or the curry-buttered bun halves (see recipe below).
0 Garnish with sprigs of fresh parsley and hot plumped prunes.

Curry-buttered buns

cooking time   few minutes

you will need:

4 soft rolls	$\frac{1}{8}$ teaspoon curry powder
2 oz. butter or margarine	

1 Halve and toast buns.
2 Combine butter and curry powder, spread on buns.

Sausage croquettes

cooking time   about 8 minutes

you will need for 4 servings:

1 lb. pork sausage meat	1 beaten egg
4 oz. chopped bacon	breadcrumbs
salt	3 oz. lard or fat
pepper	2 large cooking apples

1 Mix the sausage meat with the bacon and seasoning.
2 Form into 8 cork shapes.
3 Dip in the beaten egg and toss in breadcrumbs.
4 Fry in hot fat for about 8 minutes.
5 Core but do not peel the apples, cut into slices about $\frac{1}{3}$ inch thick and fry.
6 Serve with potato croquettes.

Devilled sausages

cooking time   few minutes

you will need for 4 servings:

1½ oz. butter or margarine	seasoning
1 teaspoon curry powder	8 oz. beef sausages
1 tablespoon chutney	fried bread or toast fingers

1 Cream butter, add curry powder, chutney and seasoning.
2 Spread over sausages.
3 Put under grill and heat thoroughly.
4 Serve on hot toast or fried bread fingers.

Sausages splits

cooking time   20–30 minutes

you will need for 4 servings:

1 lb. pork sausages	garlic salt
8 oz. mashed potato	cayenne
½–1 tablespoon horseradish sauce	**To garnish:**
1 tablespoon tomato ketchup	chopped parsley

1 Cook sausages by boiling, grilling or frying. Allow to get cold.
2 Cook potatoes and mash.
3 Beat in the horseradish sauce, ketchup, garlic salt and cayenne.
4 Put this into a forcing bag.
5 Cut each cold sausage down its length but not quite into 2 parts and open out flat on a serving dish.
6 Pipe the savoury mixture down the centre of each sausage and top with chopped parsley.
7 Serve on a salad platter.

Surprise sausages

cooking time   30 minutes

you will need for 4 servings:

4 pork sausages	2 oz. Cheddar cheese
½–1 tablespoon made mustard	4 rashers bacon
	salt and pepper

1 Slit the sausages lengthways but do not cut through.
2 Spread each slit with mustard.
3 Cut cheese into wedges and stuff a piece into each sausage.
4 Wrap each sausage in a bacon rasher, season and fasten in place with a cocktail stick.
5 Put in roasting tin, season and cover with lid or foil.
6 Bake in a moderate oven (375°F.—Gas Mark 4) for 30 minutes.
7 Serve with salad.

Savouries with Rice and Pasta

Rice and pasta are extremely sustaining, so they make a good basis for interesting and economical savouries. There are certain rules in cooking both rice and pasta which give a very much better result.

How to cook rice

1 Allow 2 pints water, 1 teaspoon salt to each 4 oz. rice. Bring the water to the boil. Add salt and rice. Cook steadily until tender. This will depend on the type of rice but test after about 12–15 minutes. Strain and if you wish to separate the grains pour either boiling or cold water through them, then spread on a flat tray to dry.

2 To each oz. of rice allow 2 fluid oz. of water (or to 1 cup rice allow 2 cups water). Put the rice, water and salt to taste in a saucepan. Bring to the boil. Stir briskly. Cover with a tightly fitting lid, lower the heat and allow to simmer for approximately 14–15 minutes, by which time the water will all be absorbed and the grains quite separate.

To cook pasta

Always allow plenty of water—you need a minimum of 2 pints to each 4 oz. pasta—with approximately 1 teaspoon salt. Add the pasta to the boiling water. Do no overcook—it is ready when it just yields to a fork against the side of the pan. Naturally tastes vary as to how soft the pasta should be, but it has more flavour if it is not too soft.

Brown rice and cheese

cooking time   35 minutes

you will need for 4 servings:

2 eggs	**To garnish:**
½ pint milk	paprika
4 oz. grated cheese	chopped parsley
seasoning	
	4 oz. cooked brown rice

1 Beat the eggs.
2 Pour on the milk, add the grated cheese and seasoning and bake for approximately 35 minutes in the centre of a moderate oven (375°F.—Gas Mark 4).
3 Garnish with chopped parsley and paprika Serve with rice.

Cream cheese noodles

cooking time   50 minutes

you will need for 4 servings:

6 oz. noodles	2 oz. butter
seasoning	2 tablespoons parsley
6–8 oz. cottage or	1 small onion, chopped
cream cheese	3 eggs
1 oz. grated Parmesan cheese	

1 Cook the noodles until tender in boiling salted water.
2 Strain.
3 Add all the other ingredients.
4 Bake in a greased casserole for approximately 30 minutes in the centre of a moderate oven (375°F.—Gas Mark 4).

Egg and savoury rice

cooking time   20 minutes

you will need for 4 servings:

3 oz. long-grain rice	4 hard-boiled eggs
salad cream (see page 91)	
1 oz. sultanas	**To garnish:**
1 teaspoon capers	watercress
lemon juice	2–4 oz. shrimps
	3 tomatoes

1 Cook the rice (see this page).
2 When hot mix with salad cream, sultanas, capers and lemon juice.
3 Cool.
4 Place in shallow dish after blending with capers and lemon juice.
5 Garnish with watercress, sliced tomatoes and shrimps.

Harlequin rice

cooking time   50 minutes—1 hour

you will need for 4 servings:

2 onions, sliced	few drops hot sauce
1 oz. dripping or fat	(chilli or Tabasco)
1 large can tomatoes	½ clove garlic, minced
½ pint apple juice or	6 oz. rice, uncooked
stock	2 tablespoons olives,
pinch salt	sliced
pinch pepper	

1 Brown onions in dripping or fat.
2 Add remaining ingredients and pour into shallow baking pan.
3 Cover.
4 Bake in a very moderate oven (350°F.—Gas Mark 3) for 40–50 minutes until rice is tender.
5 Toss rice mixture lightly with fork twice during last 20 minutes of cooking.

Kedgeree

cooking time   25–30 minutes

you will need for 4 servings:

6–8 oz. rice	2 oz. butter
12 oz. flaked cooked	2 hard-boiled eggs
white or smoked fish	seasoning
a little cream or milk	

1 Cook the rice until just tender (see page 70).
2 Strain and put into the pan with the fish, the cream and the butter.
3 Heat gently, seasoning well, then add the chopped hard-boiled egg white, pile in a hot dish, and top with the chopped yolk.

Macaroni alla bebe

cooking time   25–30 minutes

you will need for 4 servings:

6 oz. macaroni	½ pint béchamel or
about 4 oz. chopped	white sauce (see
cooked tongue*	page 91)
4 oz. chopped cooked	1–2 tablespoons cream
chicken	(optional)
2–4 oz. mushrooms	little grated cheese
1 oz. butter	

*Small lambs' tongues excellent in this recipe—you can use all ham or all tongue

1 Boil the macaroni in salted water until tender.
2 Meanwhile prepare the meat mixture.
3 Fry the chopped mushrooms in the butter, add the chopped tongue and chicken, then stir in the béchamel or white sauce.
4 Heat together, stirring well, and take care the mixture is not too thick—if necessary, add a little milk.
5 Mix with the strained macaroni, stir in a small quantity of the grated cheese and the cream.
6 Taste and re-season if necessary.
7 Put into a shallow entrée dish, sprinkle grated cheese on top and brown under a hot grill.

Macaroni with bacon and wine sauce

cooking time   15 minutes

you will need for 4 servings:

6 oz. quick-cooking	salt and pepper
macaroni	1 egg yolk
4 oz. bacon	⅛ pint cream
⅛ pint white wine	Parmesan cheese

1 Cook macaroni in boiling salted water until tender.
2 Strain.
3 Meanwhile dice and fry the bacon until just crisp, add the wine and good shake of pepper.
4 Stir in the cooked macaroni, then the well beaten egg and cream.
5 Mix thoroughly, heat gently, taste and re-season as necessary.
6 Serve with grated Parmesan cheese.

Macaroni and mushroom loaf

cooking time   50 minutes

you will need for 4 servings:

4 oz. cooked macaroni	few breadcrumbs
or spaghetti	2 tablespoons grated
2 oz. margarine	cheese
1 small onion	
2 large tomatoes	**To garnish:**
4 oz. mushrooms	cooked peas
seasoning	mushrooms
1 egg	

1 Chop the spaghetti into small lengths—the quick-cooking macaroni is an ideal length.
2 Heat the margarine and fry the finely chopped onion, sliced tomatoes and chopped mushrooms until soft.
3 Mix with the macaroni or spaghetti, seasoning, egg and enough breadcrumbs to make a sticky consistency.
4 Press into a greased loaf tin and bake in the centre of a moderate oven (375°F.—Gas Mark 4) for 40 minutes.
5 Turn out and sprinkle the grated cheese on top.
6 Garnish with peas and mushrooms.

Economical paella

cooking time   30 minutes

you will need:

1 large onion	little cooked chicken
little oil or butter	1 jar mussels
2 large tomatoes, sliced	seasoning
8 oz. rice	chopped parsley
1 pint stock, or water and chicken stock cube	

1 Peel and chop the onion finely, then fry in the hot butter or oil until transparent looking.
2 Add the sliced tomatoes, but do not cook further.
3 Put in the rice and the stock, or water and chicken stock cube.
4 Bring to the boil, then lower the heat, put a lid on the pan and cook gently for 15 minutes.
5 Remove the lid, add diced chicken and mussels —the liquid can be added if wished.
6 Heat gently with the rice for a few minutes, adding extra seasoning and parsley.

Note:

If wished about 1 teaspoon powdered saffron may be put in with the rice when cooking.

Risotto

cooking time   about 40 minute

you will need for 4 servings:

1 oz. margarine	salt
1 onion, finely chopped	ground black pepper
1 clove garlic, crushed (optional)	4 oz. cooked chicken
	2 oz. cooked ham*
6 oz. rice	2 tomatoes
1¼ pint chicken stock or water with bouillon cube	1 medium can peas
	Parmesan cheese

*If chicken omitted, allow 6 oz. ham

1 Melt the margarine in a frying pan.
2 Fry the onion and garlic lightly.
3 Add the rice and cook until all the fat is absorbed.
4 Stir in the stock and simmer gently for about 30 minutes until the rice is just cooked.
5 Season.
6 Add the chicken and ham cut into strips, the tomato, skinned, seeded and cut into strips, and drained peas.
7 Heat through and serve immediately accompanied by grated Parmesan cheese.

Rigati in creamed meat sauce

cooking time   30 minutes

you will need for 4 servings:

4–6 oz. bacon, diced	¼ pint thick cream or ¼ pint thick white sauce
1 onion, finely chopped	
1 oz. butter	
beef or chicken bouillon cube	seasoning
¼ pint hot water	6 oz. rigati or long-cut macaroni
	grated cheese

1 Fry the onion and bacon in the hot butter until golden brown.
2 Dissolve the bouillon cube in the hot water, add to the sauce or cream, stir in the bacon and seasoning and heat together.
3 Meanwhile, cook the rigati or macaroni in boiling salted water until tender, drain and mix with the sauce and some grated cheese.
4 Put into hot dish, top with more grated cheese and brown under the grill if wished.

Salmon and rice croquettes

cooking time   35–40 minutes

you will need for 4 servings:

2 tablespoons rice	2–3 tablespoons crisp breadcrumbs
1 medium can salmon	
salt	
pepper	**To garnish:**
2 teaspoons lemon juice	watercress
1 egg	lemon

1 Cook rice (see page 70).
2 Flake salmon with fork.
3 Add seasoning and lemon juice.
4 Blend well together, form into croquettes and allow to stand for 15 minutes (to settle firmly into shape).
5 Brush with egg and roll in crumbs.
6 Place in buttered ovenware dish and bake for 15–20 minutes in a moderate oven (375°F.—Gas Mark 4).
7 Garnish with watercress and lemon slices.

Spaghetti bolognese

cooking time   1 hour

you will need for 4 servings:

6–8 oz. spaghetti
grated cheese

For the sauce:
$1-1\frac{1}{2}$ oz. butter and
  1 tablespoon olive oil
  or 2 oz. butter
$\frac{1}{2}-1$ clove garlic
  (optional)
1 onion, finely chopped
4 oz. mushrooms
1 carrot, shredded

approx. 6 oz. minced
  beef
1 can tomatoes or
  1 tube or small can
  tomato purée or
  4 fresh tomatoes
seasoning
$\frac{1}{2}$ pint good brown
  stock if using tinned
  tomatoes or $\frac{5}{8}$ pint if
  using fresh tomatoes
  or purée
1 wineglass red wine

1 Heat the butter and oil in a pan, then gently fry the crushed garlic, onion, mushrooms and carrot for several minutes.
2 Add the meat and the rest of the ingredients and simmer until the sauce has thickened.
3 Cook the spaghetti in boiling salted water— the quick cooking variety takes 7 minutes.
4 Strain.
5 Pour the sauce on top and serve with grated cheese.

Note:

Although not correct, you could include a sliced red or green pepper in this sauce. A little chopped parsley can be added just before serving.

Southern casserole

cooking time   40 minutes

you will need for 4 servings:

8 oz. Cheddar cheese
8 oz. sausages
4 oz. spaghetti

can creamed sweet corn
4 oz. butter
seasoning

1 Slice cheese thinly.
2 Grill, fry or bake the sliced sausages until golden brown.
3 Meanwhile, cook the spaghetti until tender, strain, chop into neat lengths, and mix with the creamed sweet corn.
4 Season well.
5 Put a layer at the bottom of a casserole, cover with a layer of cheese, then a layer of corn mixture.
6 Top with a thick layer of cheese.

7 Cook for 15 minutes in a moderately hot oven (400°F.—Gas Mark 5).
8 Arrange hot sausages on top.

Spaghetti marinara

cooking time   20–25 minutes

you will need for 4 servings:

6 oz. spaghetti

For the sauce:
1–2 large onions
1–2 cloves garlic
tablespoon olive or
  corn oil
$\frac{1}{4}-\frac{1}{2}$ pint shrimps or
  prawns

$\frac{1}{4}$ pint Riesling or
  Graves white wine
3 large tomatoes
seasoning

To garnish:
little chopped parsley

1 Put the spaghetti into boiling salted water and boil until tender.
2 To prepare the sauce, chop the onions finely, grate or crush the garlic.
3 Fry steadily in the hot oil until golden brown.
4 Add the chopped prawns or shrimps to the onions and brown delicately—DO NOT OVERCOOK OTHERWISE THEY TOUGHEN.
5 Add the wine and tomatoes, skinned and chopped, to the prawn mixture, season and heat throughly.
6 Stir in the drained spaghetti.
7 Serve garnished with chopped parsley.

Spanish rice au gratin

cooking time   30 minutes

you will need for 6 servings:

8 oz. long-grain rice
2 oz. butter
6 oz. onion, chopped
4 oz. celery, chopped
2 small green peppers,
  seeded and sliced
1 lb. ripe tomatoes,
  skinned and sliced

salt, sugar and pinch
  chilli powder
1 teaspoon Worcester-
  shire sauce
2 tablespoons tomato
  ketchup
4 oz. cheese

1 Cook rice in boiling, salted water for 14 minutes (see page 70).
2 Meanwhile, cook onions, green pepper and celery in butter.
3 Add tomatoes, salt, sugar, chilli powder, Worcestershire sauce and ketchup.
4 Add cooked rice and simmer until thick.
5 Pour into a buttered casserole and top with cheese.
6 Place under grill and melt.

Savoury Vegetable Dishes

Vegetables are all too often considered as an accompaniment to meat or fish but in fact they make a good savoury dish by themselves, quite the best way to appreciate the true flavour of vegetables when they are in season.

Aubergines with tomatoes

cooking time   30 minutes

you will need for 4 servings:

2 large aubergines	2 tablespoons milk or
3 large tomatoes	stock
seasoning	1 oz. butter
2 tablespoons breadcrumbs	

1 Cook whole aubergines in boiling salted water until just tender.
2 Slice aubergines and tomatoes and fill a dish with alternate slices of each, seasoning well and ending with aubergines.
3 Cover with crumbs, stock or milk, and butter.
4 Bake for 15 minutes in a moderately hot oven (400–425°F.—Gas Mark 5–6).

Stuffed aubergines

cooking time   30 minutes

you will need for 4 servings:

2 medium aubergines	1 tomato
$\frac{1}{2}$ teaspoon salt	4 oz. grated Cheddar cheese
2 teaspoons corn oil	
3 oz. breadcrumbs	
2 oz. cooked ham, diced	$\frac{1}{2}$ pint cheese sauce (see page 89)
1 hard-boiled egg, chopped	1 oz. extra grated Cheddar cheese

1 Wash the aubergines and remove the stalks, then cut in half lengthwise.
2 Loosen the flesh in each aubergine half from $\frac{1}{4}$ inch from the skin and then lightly make criss-cross cuts across the surface to ensure even cooking.
3 Sprinkle with salt and corn oil.
4 Put on a greased baking tin in a moderately hot oven (400°F.—Gas Mark 5) until the centre is nearly cooked.
5 Blend breadcrumbs with all the other ingredients.

6 Scoop out about half the flesh from the centre of the cooked aubergines, chop up and add to the stuffing.
7 Fill the aubergine cases with the stuffing, sprinkle with grated cheese and return to the oven for a further 15 minutes.
8 Serve hot with cheese sauce.

Note:

When aubergines are not available, the same stuffing is delicious in red or green peppers.

Boston baked beans

cooking time $5\frac{1}{2}$ hours

you will need for 4–6 servings:

1 lb. dried haricot beans	2 tablespoons black treacle
cold water	
8 oz. fat salt pork	2 teaspoons dry mustard
1 large onion	1 teaspoon salt
1 oz. brown sugar	pepper

1 Wash beans, cover with cold water and soak overnight.
2 Drain, put into a large pan and cover with water.
3 Bring to the boil and simmer for 10 minutes.
4 Drain, reserving $\frac{1}{2}$ pint of the liquid.
5 Chop rind of pork into 1-inch squares and cut rest of meat in half.
6 Place half the pork and the onion, peeled and sliced, in a heatproof casserole, cover with the beans and add rest of pork.
7 Blend remaining ingredients with the drained liquor and pour into casserole.
8 Cover and cook in a very slow oven (275°F.—Gas Mark 1) for about $5\frac{1}{4}$ hours.
9 Stir occasionally and add more water if beans seem too dry.

Cauliflower au gratin

cooking time   30–35 minutes

you will need for 4 servings:

1 cauliflower	seasoning
4 oz. grated cheese	little milk or cream
2 oz. butter	

Cook cauliflower in boiling salted water until tender.

Drain well and beat until a soft purée.

Put half in a dish and cover with half the cheese, butter and seasoning.

Add rest of cauliflower, cheese, butter, seasoning and 2 or 3 tablespoons milk or cream.

Bake for 10–15 minutes near the top of a fairly hot oven (425°F.—Gas Mark 6).

Cauliflower garnished with egg and crumbs

cooking time　　　　　　20–25 minutes

you will need for 4 servings:

1 cauliflower	1 hard-boiled egg, chopped
4 heaped tablespoons breadcrumbs	1 tablespoon chopped parsley
2 oz. butter	

1 Break cauliflower into sprigs and boil in salted water until just tender.
2 Drain and arrange in a hot dish with all the white flowers uppermost.
3 Toss crumbs in butter until brown and crisp.
4 Mix with egg and parsley.
5 Sprinkle over cauliflower.

Creamy cauliflower with ham

cooking time　　　　　　25 minutes

you will need for 4 servings:

1 large cauliflower	1 small onion, finely grated
1 oz. butter	4 thick slices ham, diced
1 oz. flour	4 tablespoons cream
¾ pint milk	2 tablespoons mayonnaise (see page 36)
salt	
pepper	

1 Trim outer leaves from the cauliflower. Boil, whole, in salted water until tender.
2 Meanwhile, to make the sauce, melt the butter in a pan, sprinkle in the flour and gradually add the milk stirring all the time.
3 Season with salt, pepper and add onion.
4 Blend in the diced ham, cream and mayonnaise.
5 Reheat very gently, WITHOUT ALLOWING TO BOIL.
6 Drain the cauliflower well.
7 Arrange on a dish and cover with the ham sauce.
8 Serve with peas and boiled rice.

Stuffed mushrooms

cooking time　　　　　　35–40 minutes

you will need for 4 servings:

8 medium mushrooms	pinch saffron (optional)
2 oz. long-grain rice	2 oz. grated cheese
1 tablespoon oil	1 egg
1 small onion, chopped	4 slices bread
2–3 rashers streaky bacon, chopped	oil for frying

1 Skin the mushrooms, if necessary, but do not remove the stalks.
2 Cook the rice in boiling salted water until tender (see page 70).
3 Drain well.
4 Heat the oil and fry the onion and bacon, add rice and cook a further 2–3 minutes.
5 Remove from the heat and add saffron, cheese and egg.
6 Mix well.
7 Pile the stuffing mixture on to the mushrooms, arranging evenly around the stalks.
8 Place on a baking tray and bake for approximately 20 minutes in a moderate oven (375°F. —Gas Mark 4).
9 Cut the bread to the same size as the mushrooms and fry until golden brown in the heated oil.
10 Drain well on soft paper.
11 Place mushrooms on fried bread and serve.

Barbecued potatoes

cooking time　　　　　　1¼–1½ hours

you will need for 6–12 servings:

6 large potatoes	3 large tomatoes
12 middle rashers bacon	dash of Worcestershire sauce
knob butter	little made mustard
seasoning	
3–4 oz. grated Cheddar cheese	**To garnish:**
1 oz. butter or bacon fat	watercress
1 large or 2 medium onions, very thinly sliced	

1 Cook the potatoes in their jackets until soft.
2 Halve carefully and remove centre potato pulp.
3 Mash pulp, add some of seasoning, knob butter and nearly all the cheese.
4 Pile or pipe back again into potato cases, leaving a large well in the middle.
5 Sprinkle rest of cheese on top of potato.

continued on next page

6 Make 6 of the rashers into 12 small bacon rolls and put these on a skewer.
7 Put the bacon rolls and potato cases in a moderately hot oven (400°F.—Gas Mark 5) for about 10 minutes until crisp and brown.
8 Meanwhile, heat fat in pan and fry sliced onions until nearly tender.
9 Add rest of bacon—cut into thin strips—and continue frying until bacon and onions are cooked.
10 Stir in sliced tomatoes, seasoning, mustard and Worcestershire sauce, and cook gently until a soft moist mixture is formed.
11 Pile into each potato case, top with bacon rolls, garnish with watercress.

Savoury potatoes

cooking time   1¼ hours

you will need for 4 servings:

4 large potatoes	3 oz. grated cheese
	1 egg
For the filling:	salt and cayenne pepper
4 oz. raw ham	made mustard
1 small onion	1½ oz. butter or margarine

1 Cook the potatoes by washing, drying, pricking with a fork and baking for about 1 hour in a hot oven (425–450°F.—Gas Mark 6–7).
2 Put the ham and onion through a mincer and mix in 2 oz. of the cheese, the beaten egg and seasonings.
3 Cut the potatoes into halves, scoop out the pulp and mix first with the fat then with the savoury mixture.
4 Put the mixture into the potato cases.
5 Sprinkle with the rest of the cheese.
6 Wrap each potato in foil to completely cover it, then bake for another 15 minutes in the hot oven.
7 Serve at once in the foil containers.

Tomato and mushroom towers

cooking time   15 minutes

you will need for 4 servings:

8 tomatoes	5 oz. grated Cheddar cheese
2 onions	
1 oz. butter	8 large button mushrooms
seasoning	

1 Cut tops off the tomatoes and remove pulp.
2 Chop the onions and lightly fry in some of the butter.
3 Season well and mix the cheese to a paste with the tomato pulp.
4 Remove the mushroom stalks, chop and mix with the cheese paste, setting aside the whole mushrooms.
5 Place tomatoes in a fireproof dish putting cooked onion inside them.
6 Spread cheese mixture on undersides of mushrooms.
7 Sit a mushroom on top of each tomato and cover with the tomato lids.
8 Brush over with remaining butter.
9 Bake in hot oven (425–450°F.—Gas Mark 6–7) for about 15 minutes.
10 Serve immediately.

Ratatouille

cooking time   45 minutes—1 hour

you will need for 4 servings:

2 onions	a little fat bacon
1 lb. tomatoes	1–2 cloves garlic
salt	pepper
1 medium marrow	
4 small aubergines	**To garnish:**
1 red or green pepper	little chopped parsley

1 Chop the onions, skin the tomatoes and cut them in half, sprinkle with salt and leave upturned to drain.
2 Peel the marrow, cut in large chunks, remove the stalks of the aubergines and cut in chunks.
3 Seed and slice the pepper.
4 Heat the bacon fat in a strong pan and gently fry the onions and the crushed garlic.
5 Add the aubergines, marrow, tomatoes and pepper.
6 Season well and simmer slowly, with well-fitting lid on the pan, until vegetables are tender.
7 Serve sprinkled with parsley.

Making Salad Savouries

For salads, you need not adhere strictly to quantities. They provide an opportunity for mixing together those ingredients that one particularly likes. But to be sustaining, a salad should contain a protein food such as egg, cheese, meat or fish. It should also have a good selection of colourful ingredients.

Chicken almond salad

cooking time   5 minutes

you will need for 4 servings:

6 oz. seedless raisins	1 teaspoon salt
12 oz. cooked chicken	pepper
4 oz. toasted almonds	1 tablespoon lemon
1 tablespoon grated	juice
onion	2 tablespoons
1 tablespoon chopped	mayonnaise
parsley	$\frac{1}{4}$ pint thin cream

1 Plump seedless raisins by covering with cold water.
2 Bring to the boil, cover and leave to stand for 5 minutes.
3 Cut chicken into long shreds, place with all the other ingredients in a mixing bowl and mix with mayonnaise and cream just before serving.
4 Serve on a bed of lettuce with cranberry sauce.

Curried chicken salad

no cooking

you will need for 4 servings:

12 oz. cooked chicken	$\frac{1}{4}$ pint salad cream (see
3 oz. celery, diced	page 91)
4 oz. sharp apple, diced	2–3 tablespoons cream
2 teaspoons finely	salt and pepper
grated onion	2 oz. almonds, toasted
2 teaspoons curry	and chopped
powder	

1 Cut chicken into large pieces.
2 Mix with the celery, apple and onion.
3 Blend the curry with the salad cream and cream.
4 Season to taste and add the almonds.
5 Stir the chicken and vegetables into the dressing.
6 Chill before serving with lettuce and tomatoes.

Emerald salad

cooking time   few minutes

you will need for 4 servings:

1 lime jelly	1 small fresh pineapple
$\frac{1}{2}$ pint water	or $\frac{1}{2}$ large pineapple
juice $\frac{1}{2}$ lemon	1 grapefruit
12 oz. cottage cheese	1 orange
$\frac{1}{2}$ lettuce, shredded	1 box cress
	5–6 radishes

1 Dissolve lime jelly in $\frac{1}{4}$ pint of the water, heated to very hot.
2 When thoroughly dissolved stir in lemon juice and remaining $\frac{1}{4}$ pint cold water, mixing well.
3 When mixture begins to thicken, lightly fold in half the cottage cheese, but do not mix too thoroughly.
4 Fill a lightly oiled ring mould with the mixture and chill.
5 Line centre of salad platter with shredded lettuce.
6 Turn lime shape out on top, cover base of centre with shredded lettuce and fill up with cottage cheese.
7 Arrange overlapping slices of radishes round the cheese piled in the centre of the lime mould.
8 Border the mould with pieces of prepared fruit, placing a posy of cress between each little pyramid of fruit sections.

Gammon and pineapple salad

no cooking time

you will need for 4 servings:

4 oz. cooked gammon or	lettuce
ham	
1 15-oz. can pineapple	**To garnish:**
slices	pineapple
vinaigrette dressing (see	radishes
page 37)	cucumber
	anchovy fillets

1 Dice gammon and pineapple.
2 Toss in dressing to which you have added a little pineapple syrup.
3 Serve on bed of crisp lettuce.
4 Garnish with pineapple, radishes, cucumber and anchovy fillets.

Harlequin salad

no cooking time

you will need for 4 servings:

6 oz. cooked macaroni
little mustard
mayonnaise (see page 36)
4 hard-boiled eggs
3 oz. chopped ham or
  shelled shrimps
4 tomatoes
small piece cucumber or
  few chopped gherkins

1 green pepper
lettuce

To garnish:
watercress
little chopped parsley
lemon

1 Rinse cooked macaroni in cold water.
2 Allow to dry well.
3 Blend a little mustard with mayonnaise and toss macaroni in this.
4 Add chopped eggs, ham or shrimps, 2 of the tomatoes sliced thickly, the diced cucumber and sliced pepper.
5 Pile on a bed of lettuce and garnish with watercress, parsley, remaining tomatoes and lemon.

Hot potato salad

cooking time   20—25 minutes

you will need:

1½ lb. new potatoes
8 oz. French beans
2 tablespoons oil
1 tablespoon vinegar
3 tablespoons hot
  chicken stock

1 tablespoon finely
  chopped onion
4—6 rashers streaky
  bacon

1 Cook potatoes and beans separately.
2 Make a dressing from the oil, vinegar, stock and onion.
3 Dice the rashers and fry lightly.
4 Slowly add the dressing to the bacon and heat.
5 Pour this mixture over the hot, drained, sliced potatoes and beans.
6 Serve hot with cold ham, meat or poultry and a green salad.

Sundowner's hat salad

no cooking

you will need for 6 servings:

1 can pineapple slices
8 oz. grated Cheddar
  cheese
¼ teaspoon salt
⅛ teaspoon paprika

1 green pepper
1 red pepper
1 lettuce
2 tomatoes

1 Drain juice from pineapple.
2 Mix cheese and seasonings with 1 tablespoon of the juice.
3 Mould into egg cups.
4 Unmould each on to a slice of pineapple and mark top to represent dent in the crown of a hat.
5 Arrange a strip of red pepper for hatband and use green pepper for a bow.
6 Serve on lettuce leaves, garnished with tomato quarters and salad cream (see page 91).

Fried Savouries

There is a great variety of fried savouries one can make but generally speaking the rules for success are:

1 make sure the fat is sufficiently hot to set the outside of the savoury quickly. This prevents the mixture from being soggy.
2 Drain well on either kitchen paper or crumpled tissue paper.
3 Serve as quickly as possible after cooking.

Bacon beignets

cooking time   few minutes

you will need for 6—8 portions:

1 lb. cooked bacon
  (forehock, collar or
  gammon)
8 oz. plain flour
2 eggs

seasoning
1 teaspoon basil or
  marjoram
¼ pint milk
⅛ pint beer or water

1 Cut the bacon into 1-inch cubes.
2 Sieve the flour and seasoning into a bowl and add the eggs and herbs.

3 Gradually mix in the milk, then the beer or water.
4 Beat well and allow to stand for at least 1 hour.
5 Dip pieces of bacon into the batter.
6 Fry in deep, hot fat until golden brown.
7 Drain on crumpled kitchen paper.

Cheese brochettes

cooking time   3—4 minutes

you will need for 4 servings:

6 medium-thick slices bread	½ pint cheese sauce (see page 89)
1 lb. Cheddar cheese	
¼ pint milk	**For the egg dip:**
2 oz. seasoned flour	2 egg yolks
fat for frying	¼ teaspoon salt
1 lb. cooked spinach	pinch cayenne
	1 tablespoon water

1 Take six 1-inch squares of bread and five 1-inch squares of Cheddar cheese, approximately ¼ inch thick, and spear alternately on to a small skewer so that they just touch.
2 Mix together ingredients for egg dip.
3 Soak the brochettes in milk, roll in seasoned flour and then in the egg dip.
4 Fry in deep fat at a very moderate heat (i.e. when a cube of bread turns golden brown in 1 minute) until golden brown.
5 Drain and serve hot, on a bed of spinach, covered with cheese sauce.

Cheese meringues

cooking time   2—3 minutes

you will need for 4 servings:

2 egg whites	fat or oil for frying
seasoning	
2 oz. finely grated cheese, preferably Parmesan	**To garnish:** parsley watercress

1 Whisk egg whites until very stiff.
2 Fold in seasoning and cheese.
3 Drop spoonfuls into hot oil or fat and fry until crisp and brown.
4 Drain and serve at once.
5 Garnish with parsley or watercress.

Fried cheese sandwiches

cooking time   few minutes

you will need for 4 servings:

8 large thin slices wholemeal bread	2 oz. butter for frying
8 oz. Cheddar cheese, thinly sliced	**To garnish:** 2 tomatoes
4 teaspoons chutney	

1 Cover the bread slices with the cheese, and spread over a little chutney.
2 Put two cheese-covered slices together and press firmly.
3 Cut into neat shapes and fry to a crisp golden brown on both sides in butter.
4 Serve hot, garnished with tomato slices.

Making fritters

Fritters are quick to prepare and cook, and can easily be varied. Here are some suggestions:

Diced ham Mix approximately 8 oz. diced ham with batter (see Corned beef, page 80) and fry in spoonfuls.

Cheese Dip slices or portions of cheese in batter, fry for 1 minute (see page 80).

Fish Mix about 6—8 oz. well drained flaked cooked fish in batter, fry in spoonfuls for few minutes.

Roe Separate cooked soft or hard herring roes or dice cod's roe. Coat in batter and fry until crisp and golden brown.

Carrot Cooked young carrots can be coated in plain or cheese-flavoured batter and fried steadily until crisp and golden brown.

Cauliflower fritters

cooking time   few minutes

you will need for 4 servings:

1 cooked cauliflower	paprika
1 egg	1 oz. melted butter
2½ tablespoons milk and water	oil or fat for frying
2 oz. flour	
seasoning	**To garnish:** chopped parsley

1 Divide cooked cauliflower into sprigs.
2 Make batter by mixing egg yolk and milk with seasoned flour, then fold in the melted butter and stiffly beaten egg whites.
3 Dip cauliflower sprigs in this.
4 Fry in hot fat until crisp and golden brown.
5 Drain and garnish with parsley.

Corned beef fritters

cooking time   5—8 minutes

you will need for 4 servings:

For the batter:	seasoning
4 oz. flour (plain or self-raising)	
1 egg	12 oz. corned beef
¼ pint milk	fat for frying

1 Make the batter by blending the egg with the seasoned flour then adding the milk gradually.
2 Slice the corned beef thinly and coat carefully with the batter.*
3 Put into hot fat and fry steadily until the fritters are crisp and brown on the outside and the meat very hot inside.
4 Serve the fritters with salad or with fried onion rings and vegetables.

*If preferred the corned beef can be flaked and mixed with the batter, then drop spoonfuls of the mixture into the hot fat

Cheese fritters

cooking time   8 minutes

you will need for 4 servings:

4 oz. flour (with plain flour use 1 teaspoon baking powder)	seasoning
	4 oz. finely grated cheese
1 egg	oil or fat for frying
¼ pint milk	

1 Make a thick batter with the flour, egg and milk.
2 Season well and add the grated cheese.
3 Drop in small spoonfuls in hot oil or fat and fry until crisp and golden brown.

Quick macaroni fritters

cooking time   5 minutes

you will need for 4 servings:

2 oz. macaroni	little fat for frying
3 eggs	1 packet mushroom soup
4 oz. grated cheese	¼ pint water
seasoning	½ pint milk

1 Cook macaroni in plenty of boiling salted water until tender.
2 Drain well.
3 Beat together eggs, cheese and seasoning.
4 Mix in macaroni.
5 Heat fat in frying pan and drop in spoonfuls of the mixture.

6 Fry until crisp and golden, turn and brown other side.
7 Drain and serve with a mushroom sauce made by heating mushroom soup with water and milk.

Cheeseolettes

cooking time   few minutes

you will need for 4 servings:

3 eggs	1 tablespoon grated onion
2 oz. flour (with plain flour use ½ teaspoon baking powder)	2 tablespoons chopped parsley
4 oz. grated Cheddar cheese	seasoning
	fat or oil for frying

1 Blend all the ingredients together.
2 Heat the fat in pan and drop in spoonfuls of this mixture.
3 Fry until crisp and golden brown.
4 Turn, brown on the other side.
5 Drain well and serve with a dish of sliced tomatoes and another of crisp lettuce.

Pancake dishes to make

Pancake batter

cooking time   few minutes

you will need for 4 servings:

4 oz. flour, preferably plain	½ pint milk, or milk and water
pinch salt	oil or fat for frying
2 eggs	

1 Sieve flour into a bowl and add salt.
2 Make a well in the centre and stir in one egg and half the milk beaten together.
3 Beat lightly with a wooden spoon for a few minutes.
4 Add the remaining egg whisked together with the rest of the milk and mix well until batter is perfectly smooth.
5 Cover bowl and allow to stand in a cool place for 1 hour before using if possible.
6 Melt the oil or fat in a thick frying pan to coat bottom and when very hot pour off any excess.
7 Pour about 2 tablespoons of the batter into the pan and cook over medium heat until set.
8 Turn and cook other side until a golden brown.
9 Repeat until all batter is used.

18 simple fillings for pancakes

- thick cheese sauce (see page 89)
- diced bacon and tomatoes
- diced ham heated in white, cheese or tomato sauce (see pages 89–91)
- diced chicken heated in white, béchamel, or cheese sauce (see pages 89–91)
- prawns, or shrimps, heated in white, cheese, béchamel or hollandaise sauce (see pages 89–91)
- creamy spinach purée
- cooked asparagus tips
- hot sausages
- mixed cooked vegetables in thick white, cheese or tomato sauce (see pages 89–91)

Prawn and mushroom pancakes

cooking time   15 minutes

you will need for 4 servings:

½ pint pancake batter (see page 80)	½ pint milk
fat or oil for frying	seasoning
	little lemon juice
	2–3 oz. shelled prawns
For the filling:	2 oz. button or chopped
1½ oz. butter	mushrooms
1 oz. flour	little butter for frying

1 Prepare pancake batter.
2 Heat fat or oil and cook pancake quickly until the underside is golden brown. Toss and cook the other side.
3 Put on to a piece of greaseproof paper.
4 Keep the pancakes in a warm place between layers of greaseproof paper* until the filling is ready.
5 For the filling melt the butter in a saucepan over a low heat, add the flour and cook gently for a minute stirring all the time.
6 Gradually add the liquid, still stirring, until the mixture thickens.
7 Season and add lemon juice, prawns, and lightly fried mushrooms.
8 Cook for a few minutes more, then spoon on to pancakes, roll them up, and warm them in a cool oven if necessary.
9 Serve with lemon slices and garnish with more prawns.

Variation:

Vary the filling by adding chicken, sweet corn, peppers or ham to the basic sauce.

* On uncovered dish in a slow oven or over pan boiling water

Savoury Scotch pancakes

cooking time   4 minutes

you will need for 4 servings:

4 oz. flour (with plain flour use either 2 teaspoons baking powder or ½ small teaspoon bicarbonate of soda and 1 small teaspoon cream of tartar)	pinch salt, pepper and mustard
	1 egg
	¼ pint milk
	1 oz. melted margarine (optional)

1 Sieve together all the dry ingredients.
2 Beat in first the egg, then the milk.
3 Stir in the melted margarine if used.
4 Grease and warm the griddle, electric hot plate or frying pan. It is best to use the middle of the pan—the part that touches the heat.
5 To test for correct temperature, drop 1 teaspoon of the mixture on to this; if it goes brown within 1 minute, the plate is ready.
6 Drop spoonfuls of the batter on to the plate.
7 Cook for about 2 minutes.
8 Turn with a palette knife and cook the other side.
9 Press firmly with the back of a knife; if no batter comes from the sides and the pancakes feel firm, they are ready.
10 Cool on a wire tray.
These are delicious topped with butter and cheese, with cream cheese and jam, or with hot sausages and crisp bacon.

Variations:

Caraway pancakes
Add 1 teaspoon caraway seeds—particularly good topped with cream cheese.

Tomato Scotch pancakes
Blend with tomato juice instead of milk.

Cheese Scotch pancakes
1–2 oz. finely grated Parmesan cheese can be added.

Onion Scotch pancakes
Fry 1 grated onion in a little hot margarine. Add to flour and omit 1 tablespoon milk.

Savouries with Pastry

A savoury flan, tart or pastry is likely to be an extremely popular dish and as such is ideal for a number of occasions, including picnics, so I have included, at the end of this chapter, tips for carrying savouries on picnics.

How to make the pastry

Flaky pastry

cooking time   as individual recipe

you will need for 4 servings:

8 oz. plain flour   water
pinch salt
5–6 oz. fat ($\frac{1}{3}$ cooking fat and $\frac{2}{3}$ margarine, or all butter or all margarine)

1 Sieve flour with salt.
2 Mix fat and divide into 3 portions.
3 Rub one portion into flour in the usual way and mix to rolling consistency with cold water.
4 Roll out to oblong shape.
5 Take the second portion of fat, divide it into small pieces and lay them on surface of $\frac{1}{3}$ of dough, leaving remaining $\frac{2}{3}$ without fat.
6 Fold $\frac{1}{3}$ without fat on to $\frac{1}{3}$ with fat, then fold other $\frac{1}{3}$ over—to form an open envelope.
7 Turn pastry at right angles, seal open ends and 'rib' it (press with the rolling pin at intervals to give a corrugated effect and equalize the distribution of trapped air). This makes sure that the pastry will rise evenly.
8 Repeat the process again using the remaining fat and turning pastry in same way.
9 If the consistency is still firm, roll out pastry once more, but should it begin to feel very soft and sticky first put it into a cold place for 30 minutes to become firm before rolling out.
10 Fold pastry as before, turn it, seal edges and 'rib' it. Altogether the pastry should have 3 foldings and 3 rollings.
11 Then stand in a cold place for a little while before baking, since the contrast between the cold and the heat of the oven makes the pastry rise better.
12 To bake use a very hot oven (475°F.—Gas Mark 8) then lower heat to Gas Mark 6 or turn the electric oven off to finish cooking for remaining time at lower temperature.

Puff pastry

cooking time   as individual recipe

you will need:

8 oz. plain flour   cold water to mix
7–8 oz. butter or margarine or $\frac{2}{3}$ margarine and $\frac{1}{3}$ whipped up cooking fat
good pinch salt
few drops lemon juice

1 Sieve the flour and salt together.
2 Mix to rolling consistency with cold water and lemon juice.
3 Roll to oblong shape.
4 Make fat into neat block and place in centre of pastry.
5 Fold over first the bottom section of pastry to cover the fat, then the top section over this.
6 Turn the dough at right angles, seal the edges and 'rib' carefully (press with the rolling pin at intervals to give a corrugated effect and equalize distribution of trapped air). This makes sure that the pastry will rise evenly.
7 Roll out the pastry.
8 Fold into envelope again, turn to right again, seal edges, 'rib' and roll.
9 Repeat 5 times, making 7 rollings and 7 foldings in all. It will be necessary to put the pastry to rest in a cold place once or twice between rollings to prevent it becoming sticky and soft.
10 Always put it to rest before rolling for the last time, and before baking.
11 Bake in a very hot oven (to make it rise, and keep in the fat).
12 Bake for the first 10–15 minutes in a very hot oven (475–500°F.—Gas Mark 8–9) then lower to moderately hot (400°F.—Gas Mark 5). Well made puff pastry should rise to 4–5 times its original thickness.

Short crust pastry

cooking time   as individual recipe

you will need:

8 oz. flour
good pinch salt
4 oz. fat (equal quantities margarine or butter and cooking fat or lard)
approximately 2 tablespoons cold water

1 Sieve flour and salt together and rub in fat until mixture looks like fine breadcrumbs.
2 Using first a knife and then fingertips so that you can feel the texture of the pastry, gradually add enough of the cold water to mix the dough to a rolling consistency.
3 Lightly flour the rolling pin and pastry board —if a great deal of flour is necessary to roll out the pastry, then you have used too much water.
4 Roll out to required thickness and shape, lifting and turning it to keep light.
5 Exact cooking times for pastry are given in the recipes, but as a general rule it should be cooked in a hot oven (425–450°F.—Gas Mark 6–7).

Vol au vent cases 1

cooking time   15–30 minutes
you will need for 6–8 large cases*:

1 1-lb. packet frozen   made with 8 oz. flour
   pastry or puff pastry   (see page 82)

1 Roll out the puff pastry to $\frac{1}{2}$ inch thickness, keeping the rolling pin straight across. If the pastry is in just the right condition for rolling, you will need little, if any, flour on the board or rolling pin.
2 Cut into rounds.
3 Cut the centres out of half the rounds to form rings.
4 Place these rings on top of complete rounds.
5 Seal edges and put on to DAMP baking trays.
6 Glaze with beaten egg.
7 Bake in a very hot oven (475°F.—Gas Mark 8) until well risen and brown, then reduce heat slightly to make sure pastry is cooked—this will vary from 15–30 minutes according to size.

*Or 12 medium, or 36 cocktail cases

Vol au vent cases 2

cooking time   15–30 minutes
you will need for 6–8 large cases*:

1 1-lb. packet frozen
   puff pastry or puff pastry
   made with 8 oz. flour
   (see page 82)

1 Roll out the puff pastry as in Vol au vent 1 but to $\frac{3}{4}$–1 inch thickness, and cut into rounds.
2 Put on to DAMP baking trays.
3 With a smaller cutter press half way through pastry.

4 Glaze with beaten egg.
5 Bake in a very hot oven (475°F.—Gas Mark 8) until well risen and brown, then reduce heat slightly to make sure pastry is cooked.
6 Lift out the centre portion—this is quite easy to do with the point of a sharp knife—and return to the oven for a short time to dry out.

*Or 12 medium, or 36 cocktail cases

Fillings for vols au vent

Fill with either fish, chicken, mushrooms or a selection of vegetables mixed in a thick white sauce or mayonnaise.

To serve vols au vent hot

1 Bake the pastry cases and keep warm.
2 Make the fillings and keep warm.
3 Put the 2 together and serve at once.

To serve vols au vent cold

1 Allow both pastry and filling to become cold.
2 Put together and serve.

How to make a flan case

1 Use either a proper flan ring on a baking sheet, or a sandwich tin, or a deep pie plate.
2 Use either short crust pastry, or cheese pastry, using the short crust recipe (see page 82) and adding 4 oz. grated cheese.
3 It is traditional for a savoury flan to be made in a plain and not a fluted flan case, although this is not very important.
4 Roll out the pastry to slightly larger than the ring or tin.
5 Lift it without breaking by folding over the rolling pin.
6 Put flan ring on to the upturned baking tin—this makes flan easier to slide off—grease ring or tin very lightly.
7 Place the pastry over the ring or case. Press down gently but firmly at the bottom and then at the sides.
8 Cut away surplus pastry at the top being careful not to drag and stretch the pastry. Alternatively roll over with a rolling pin—if you do this firmly, and the edge of the tin is reasonably sharp, you can cut away any surplus pastry quickly and efficiently.

To bake 'blind'

To bake a pastry case 'blind' means to bake it without a filling. As there is a tendency for the pastry to rise if not weighted down by a filling, it is advisable to use plain flour. Also you can either prick the pastry well with a fork, or put a piece of greased greaseproof paper or foil inside, and cover with crusts of bread or dry haricot beans to weight down the bottom. Bake for about 15 minutes in a hot oven (425°F.—Gas Mark 6) then lift out the beans and paper and, if using a flan ring, take this away, so the outside edge of the pastry will crisp. Allow a further 5–10 minutes in the oven.

Asparagus and hollandaise flan

cooking time	25 minutes

you will need for 4 servings:

Onion pastry:	8 oz. cooked asparagus
3 oz. butter or margarine	or 1 can asparagus tips
6 oz. plain flour	**mock hollandaise**
$\frac{1}{2}$ teaspoon salt	**sauce:**
1 tablespoon grated onion	1 oz. butter
2 tablespoons cold water	1 oz. flour
	$\frac{1}{2}$ pint milk
	salt and pepper
	2 egg yolks
For the filling:	3 oz. butter
4 hard-boiled eggs	1 tablespoon lemon juice

1 Make the pastry by rubbing fat into sifted flour and salt.
2 Add onion and mix to stiff paste with the water.
3 Knead and roll out slightly larger than 8 or 9-inch pie plate.
4 Fit into plate, trim and flute edges.
5 Bake 'blind' (see above) in centre of a hot oven (425–450°F.—Gas Mark 6–7) for 20–25 minutes, until inside is golden and crisp.
6 Roll out trimmings, cut into small rounds and bake for 10 minutes only to use for garnish.
7 While flan is cooking make the white sauce with butter, flour and milk. Then while still warm and just before serving, stir in the two beaten egg yolks, the 3 oz. butter, a teaspoon at a time, and finally the lemon juice.
8 Season well.
9 Fill baked pastry case with thoroughly chopped hard-boiled eggs.
10 Pour sauce over chopped eggs and garnish with the cooked or canned asparagus placed like spokes of a wheel, tips outwards.
11 Place little pastry rounds between the asparagus groups and serve at once. A crisp green salad will make a good accompaniment.

Variations:

Salmon and hollandaise flan
Use medium can of salmon and put this in flan case with hard-boiled eggs.

Broccoli and hollandaise flan
Use cooked broccoli instead of asparagus.

Bacon and cheese flan

cooking time	40–45 minutes

you will need for 4 servings:

4 oz. short crust pastry (see page 82)	3 oz. grated cheese
6–8 rashers streaky bacon	pinch salt
1 egg	pinch cayenne
	$\frac{1}{4}$ pint top of milk or evaporated milk

1 Line a 7-inch flan ring or tin with the pastry.
2 Remove the rind from the bacon, cut 4 rashers into thin strips and fry lightly.
3 Beat the egg, add the cheese, seasonings and milk.
4 Place some cooked bacon in the flan and pour the cheese mixture over.
5 Bake in moderate oven (375°F.—Gas Mark 4) for 30 minutes.
6 Remove from the oven and garnish with the remaining bacon.
7 Return to oven and cook for further 10 minutes.
8 Serve hot or cold.

Beef and vegetable flan

cooking time	25 minutes

you will need for 4 servings:

8-inch short crust flan case (see page 82)	1 teaspoon cornflour
1 can stewed steak, or stewed steak and vegetable casserole	**To garnish:**
	1–2 tomatoes
	1 hard-boiled egg

1 Cook the flan case until crisp and golden brown.
2 Meanwhile, heat the casserole, blending in the cornflour to thicken gravy.
3 Pile into hot case.*
4 Garnish with slices of tomato and hard-boiled egg.
5 Serve hot.

   * If you prefer to serve cold, put the casserole mixture into cold pastry case. In this way you keep the pastry crisp. For special occasions, make up a small quantity of savoury jelly (see below) and brush over the top of the flan to give an attractive glaze

To make savoury jelly:

Add enough beef bouillon cube to $\frac{1}{4}$ pint water to give good beef flavour. Dissolve 1 teaspoon gelatine in the very hot liquid. Allow to set lightly, then spoon over the cold meat filling.

Cheese and onion roll

cooking time   35–40 minutes

you will need for 4 servings:

1 large onion, finely chopped	1 teaspoon chopped parsley
2 oz. butter	salt and pepper
2 oz. white breadcrumbs	4 oz. flaky or puff pastry (see page 82)
4 oz. grated Cheddar cheese	1 egg

1 Cook the onion in butter until transparent.
2 Stir in the breadcrumbs, toss in pan until crisp and remove from heat.
3 Add the cheese, parsley and seasoning to taste.
4 Roll out pastry to an oblong about 10 inches by 6 inches.
5 Brush edges with beaten egg.
6 Spread filling over pastry, roll up from short side and seal the edges.
7 Brush over with egg.
8 Bake in a hot oven (450°F.—Gas Mark 7) for 15 minutes.
9 Reduce heat to moderate (375°F.—Gas Mark 4) for 15 minutes.
10 Serve hot or cold.

Cheese soufflé tarts

cooking time   12–15 minutes

you will need for 4 servings:

4 oz. short crust pastry (see page 82)	pinch pepper
2 eggs	$\frac{1}{2}$ teaspoon chopped parsley
2 oz. finely grated Cheddar cheese	
pinch cayenne	**To garnish:**
good pinch salt	watercress

1 Roll out the pastry very thinly and line 9–12 patty tins.
2 Beat the egg yolks with the cheese and seasonings, add the parsley and lastly the stiffly beaten egg whites.
3 Put into the pastry cases and bake for approximately 12–15 minutes in the centre of a very hot oven (475–500°F.—Gas Mark 8–9).
4 Serve hot or cold garnished with watercress.

Corned beef pasties

cooking time   45 minutes

you will need for 4 servings:

1 12-oz. can corned beef	12 oz. short crust pastry
large potato	little milk or beaten egg
large onion	
seasoning	
a little stock, flavoured with beef or chicken bouillon cube	**To serve:** salad beetroot

1 Flake the corned beef and mix with GRATED raw potato and GRATED raw onion.
2 Season well and add enough stock to give a moist texture (do not make it too wet otherwise the pastry will be spoiled).
3 Roll out the pastry and cut into large rounds.
4 Put a good spoonful of the mixture into the centre of each round, fold over and flute edges firmly together. The pasties should have the traditional Cornish pasty shape.
5 Brush the pastry with milk or a little beaten egg, lift carefully on to baking tins and cook for 20 minutes in the centre of a hot oven (425–450°F.—Gas Mark 6–7).
6 Lower the heat and cook for a further 20 minutes to make sure the filling is hot and the potato and onion cooked.
7 Serve with salad and sliced beetroot.

Harlequin flan

cooking time   40—45 minutes

you will need for 4 servings:

6 oz. short crust pastry (see page 82)	selection of cooked vegetables—diced young carrots, turnips, beans, peas, beetroot and raw tomato, cucumber
2 eggs	
$\frac{3}{8}$ pint milk	
seasoning	
	4 oz. grated cheese

1 Line a deep flan ring or oblong tin with pastry, bake 'blind' for 10–15 minutes in a hot oven (425–450°F.—Gas Mark 6–7).
2 Meanwhile beat the eggs, add warm milk and seasoning.
3 Arrange the vegetables in the flan.
4 Stir cheese into custard and pour over the vegetables.
5 Bake for about 30 minutes in moderate oven (375°F.—Gas Mark 4) until filling is firm.
6 Serve hot or cold.

Quiche Lorraine or cheese flan

cooking time   30—35 minutes

you will need for 4 servings:

4 oz. bacon rashers	$\frac{1}{4}$ pint milk
6 oz. short crust or flaky pastry (see page 82)	$\frac{1}{4}$ pint cream
	2 eggs
	seasoning
6 oz. grated cheese	

1 Chop bacon finely and fry very lightly.
2 Line a really deep flan tin with pastry.
3 Beat eggs, add cream, milk, grated cheese, bacon and seasoning.
4 Pour in to flan carefully and bake in centre of a moderately hot oven (400°F.—Gas Mark 5) until the pastry is brown and the filling firm.

Note:

For a more economical flan, use more milk and egg yolks only.

Nutty Cheddar horns

cooking time   17 minutes

you will need for 9 horns:

1 lb. plain flour	**For the filling:**
$\frac{1}{4}$ teaspoon salt	8 oz. grated Cheddar cheese
1 teaspoon baking powder	$1\frac{1}{2}$ tablespoons mayonnaise (see page 36)
2 oz. butter	
scant $\frac{1}{2}$ pint milk	
1 egg	pinch cayenne
	4 pickled walnuts

1 Sieve flour, salt and baking powder into bowl.
2 Rub in butter and mix to a fairly stiff dough with the milk.
3 Roll into oblong 12×9 inches and cut into strips 1×12 inches.
4 Damp edge of strips and coil round cream horn tins.
5 Brush with beaten egg and stand on greased baking sheet.
6 Bake in a moderately hot oven (400°F.—Gas Mark 5) for 12 minutes.
7 Remove tins and bake for a further 5 minutes.
8 Allow to cool.
9 Blend grated cheese, mayonnaise and cayenne pepper.
10 Chop walnuts coarsely and fold into cheese mixture.
11 Fill horn cases with cheese filling.

Leek flan

cooking time   30—40 minutes

you will need for 4 servings:

1 lb. leeks	2 tablespoons milk
For the pastry:	2 tablespoons cream
1 oz. butter	seasoning
4 oz. flour	4 rashers streaky bacon
seasoning	4 oz. cheese
1 egg	

1 Chop the leeks and boil until tender.
2 Rub the butter into the flour sifted with the seasoning.
3 Stir in the beaten egg and enough milk to make a soft dough.
4 Roll out and press the dough into a greased 6-inch sandwich tin or flan ring.
5 Mix the cream with the leeks and seasoning and spread over the dough.
6 Lay the bacon strips on top and cover with the cheese.
7 Bake in centre of a moderately hot oven (400°F.—Gas Mark 5) for 30 minutes.

Savoury egg flan

cooking time   25 minutes

you will need for 4 servings:

6 oz. short or cheese crust pastry (see page 82)	squeeze lemon juice
	3 hard-boiled eggs
	3 tomatoes
$\frac{1}{2}$ pint water and 1 beef stock cube or $\frac{1}{2}$ pint stock	
	To garnish:
$\frac{1}{4}$ oz. gelatine	lettuce

1 Roll out pastry, line a 7-inch flan ring and bake 'blind' in hot oven (425–450°F.—Gas Mark 6–7) for about 20 minutes—until crisp and golden brown.

2 Crumble beef extract cube and dissolve in ¼ pint hot water.

3 Add gelatine and when completely dissolved, add lemon juice and ¼ pint cold water; leave in a cool place.

4 Fill flan case with quartered hard-boiled eggs and skinned and quartered tomatoes.

5 When savoury jelly is just setting, spoon mixture over the eggs and tomatoes, filling the flan.

6 Allow any surplus jelly to set and serve chopped with the flan on a lettuce bed.

Savoury flan

| cooking time | 30–35 minutes |

you will need for 4 servings:

7 oz. plain flour	½ green or red pepper
2 oz. soya flour	2 oz. mushrooms
salt	2 oz. chopped bacon
2 tablespoons soya oil	2 oz. tomatoes
2 oz. grated cheese	seasoning
little egg	1 large egg
water	4 tablespoons milk
	1 oz. grated cheese

For the filling:
½ large onion, chopped

1 Make the pastry by placing the flours and salt into a mixing bowl and adding the soya oil and cheese.

2 Mix together, add a little beaten egg and enough water to form into a pastry dough.

3 Roll the pastry out thinly.

4 Grease an 8–9 inch flan ring or pie plate and line with pastry.

5 Mince or chop together coarsely the onion, pepper, mushrooms, bacon and tomatoes.

6 Add seasoning, egg and milk and pour this mixture into the pastry case.

7 Sprinkle with grated cheese and cook for 30–35 minutes in a moderately hot oven (400°F.—Gas Mark 5).

8 This flan can be served either hot or cold.

Soufflé tarts

| cooking time | 15 minutes |

you will need for 4 servings:

4 oz. short crust pastry (see page 82)	2 teaspoons finely chopped parsley
3 tablespoons Gruyère or Parmesan cheese, grated	3 eggs
	1 teaspoon grated onion
	seasoning

1 Line tins with thin pastry.

2 Mix well beaten eggs with most of the cheese, the onion, parsley and seasoning.

3 Put spoonfuls of the filling into the pastry, scatter more grated cheese over the top and bake in centre of a hot oven (450°F.—Gas Mark 7) for 15 minutes.

Bread and scone dishes
Pizza

| cooking time | 1 hour |

you will need for 4 servings:

½ oz. yeast	1 clove garlic, chopped
1 dessertspoon tepid water	1 can anchovies
1 lb. plain flour	4 oz. Parmesan or Cheddar cheese
¼ pint water	salt and pepper
4 tablespoons olive oil	few black olives
1 lb. or 1 can tomatoes	

1 Dissolve the yeast in tepid water.

2 Mix the flour with 1 tablespoon of the olive oil, then add the dissolved yeast and water.

3 Knead until dough is smooth.

4 Leave it in a covered bowl for 2 hours.

5 Peel and chop the fresh tomatoes, or drained canned tomatoes, and put them in a pan with rest of oil and garlic.

6 Season with salt and pepper and simmer gently for 30 minutes.

7 Add the anchovies and most of the cheese when tomatoes are almost cooked.

8 When the dough has risen, roll it until it is very thin and spread it over a large, well oiled baking tin.

9 Cover it with tomato mixture and bake in centre of a hot oven (425–450°F.—Gas Mark 6–7) for approximately 25 minutes.

10 Top with rest of grated cheese and black olives.

Cocktail pizza tarts

1 Mix up half the quantity of the tomato mixture (step 5).
2 Roll out 6 oz. quantity of short crust pastry (see page 82) and make about 24 tiny tartlet cases, baking until crisp and brown.
3 Fill with the tomato mixture, top with cheese and tiny pieces of olive or anchovy fillets.

5 minute pizzas

cooking time   1 minute

you will need for 4 servings:

4 soft rolls   16 anchovy fillets
butter, optional   few olives
8 slices cheese

1 Halve the soft rolls, butter if wished.
2 Put the slices of cheese on top with the anchovy fillets in a cross and decorate with sliced olives.
3 Put under the grill for 1 minute only.

Quick pizza scones

cooking time   30 minutes

you will need for 4 servings:

For the dough:
1 lb. self-raising flour
1 teaspoon salt
2 teaspoons baking powder
3 oz. margarine
2 medium eggs
½ pint less 4 tablespoons milk

1 clove garlic, finely chopped
4 tablespoons tomato purée
½ teaspoon dried oregano (optional)
salt and pepper
3 oz. finely grated cheese*

For the sauce:
2 tablespoons oil
1 medium onion, finely chopped

anchovy fillets
halved stuffed olives

*Parmesan will give extra strong flavour

1 Sift dry dough ingredients into bowl.
2 Rub in fat to fine breadcrumbs consistency.
3 Mix to a soft dough with lightly beaten egg and milk and knead lightly until smooth.
4 If scones are not wanted until later, place dough in a polythene bag and keep in refrigerator or cool larder until ready to bake.
5 Heat oil, add onion and garlic and cook slowly till soft but not brown.
6 Stir in tomato purée and seasonings and remove from heat.

7 Turn the dough on to a lightly floured board and roll out to ½–¾ inch thick.
8 Cut into 8 rounds with a 3-inch cutter.
9 Place the rounds on a greased and floured baking tray, allowing room between each for spreading.
10 Make a 'well' in each round with the floured base of a jam jar or tumbler about 2½ inches across.
11 Fill each 'well' with the tomato sauce and cover with grated cheese.
12 Top with anchovy fillets and halved stuffed olives.
13 Bake near the top of a hot oven (425°F.—Gas Mark 7) for about 20 minutes and serve at once.

Potato cheese scones

cooking time   10–15 minutes

you will need for 4 servings:

1 teaspoon yeast extract
6 fl. oz. milk and water
2 oz. instant mashed potato powder or 4–6 oz. cooked potato
4 oz. plain flour and 2 teaspoons baking powder, or 4 oz. self-raising flour and 1 teaspoon baking powder

2 oz. melted butter or margarine
2 oz. processed cheese, finely diced
1 egg

1 Heat the yeast extract with the milk and water, then stir in the instant mashed potato powder.
2 Cool slightly, add the flour, melted butter and cheese.
3 Mix well, then add enough beaten egg to give a stiff mixture.
4 Roll out to about ¾ inch thick on a well floured pastry board.
5 Cut into rounds or triangles.
6 Brush with rest of egg to give an attractive glaze, and bake near the top of a hot oven (450–475°F.—Gas Mark 7–8) for approximately 10–12 minutes.
7 These are delicious sandwiched together with butter and processed cheese, and served with a salad.
To reheat: split, top with processed sliced cheese and put under grill for 1 minute.

10 Tips for Carrying Food on Picnics

● Make use of foil or plastic bags to keep food intact, and to prevent containers becoming sticky and heavy.

● Don't plan too 'starchy' a meal. Have such foods as fruit and salad and avoid over-sweet 'sticky' buns, cakes and things that break easily, otherwise the family will become sleepy and slightly irritable.

● Make use of waxed cartons with tightly fitting lids (or washed ice cream cartons) for potato or Russian salad, fresh fruit salad, etc.

● Wide-topped vacuum flasks can turn a picnic into a feast. Use them for hot dishes such as soups, stews (fricassée of veal, curry, etc.), milk puddings for younger children, baby's dinner. They are also useful for cold dishes such as stewed fruit, fruit salad, mixed salads and ice cream, or for cold drinks. Never put lumps of ice in vacuum flasks, as shaking might cause the flask to break. Chill the drink and blend with crushed ice, then pour into vacuum flask.

● Carry meat and fruit patties or pies in the tin in which they were cooked, or bake in aluminium foil dishes which are light AND give excellent cooking results.

● Use tubes of mustard and mayonnaise which take up little space in the hamper.

● For a picnic that you travel to by bus or on foot, pack food in individual plastic bags, so each member of the family carries his own; shell hard-boiled eggs and season all food well so you need not take seasoning.

● For a car picnic be more ambitious with savoury galantines, pies and flans, which can be transported in foil containers or UNBREAKABLE MOULDS—pack articles round with paper so they do not tip and spill.

● Take damp face flannels or sponge in plastic bag to 'freshen up' after the meal.

● Take all your left over bags, bottles and containers HOME if you can't find waste bins.

Sauces for Savoury Snacks

Anchovy sauce

cooking time   8 minutes

you will need:

1 oz. butter	chopped anchovies or
1 oz. flour	1 teaspoon anchovy
½ pint milk	essence
	salt and pepper

1 Heat the butter gently.
2 Remove from the heat and stir in the flour.
3 Return to the heat and cook without browning.
4 Again remove the pan from the heat and gradually blend in the cold milk.
5 Bring to the boil and cook, stirring with a wooden spoon, until smooth; if any lumps have formed remove by whisking sharply.
6 Add the chopped anchovies or anchovy essence, taste and season well.

Cheese sauce

cooking time   8 minutes

you will need:

1 oz. butter	3–6 oz. grated cheese
1 oz. flour	little dry mustard
½ pint milk	salt and pepper

1 Heat the butter gently.
2 Remove from the heat and stir in the flour.
3 Return to the heat and cook gently for a few minutes so that it does not brown.
4 Again remove the pan from the heat and gradually blend in the cold milk.
5 Bring to the boil and cook, stirring with a wooden spoon until smooth, whisking sharply to prevent any small lumps forming.
6 Add the grated cheese, mustard and seasoning. Serve with vegetable dishes.

Béchamel sauce

cooking time   18 minutes

you will need:

ingredients as for white   small piece celery
    sauce (see page 91)   small piece very finely
small piece carrot   chopped onion

1 Soak the vegetables in the warm milk for 10 minutes. Strain.
2 Follow method for white sauce, using the flavoured milk.

Cranberry sauce

cooking time   10—15 minutes

you will need:

12 oz. cranberries   1 tablespoon port or
3 oz. sugar   sherry, optional
2 tablespoons water

1 Heat water and sugar together.
2 Add the fruit and cook until tender.
3 Add port or sherry if wished.

French dressing

no cooking

you will need:

½—1 teaspoon English   1 tablespoon finely
    or French mustard   chopped parsley or
pinch sugar, salt and   chives
    pepper   1 tablespoon salad oil
                                 1 dessertspoon vinegar

1 Mix the dry ingredients together in a basin or on a saucer.
2 Add the oil and vinegar and mix together very thoroughly.

Hollandaise sauce

cooking time   10—15 minutes

you will need:

2 egg yolks   1—2 tablespoons lemon
pinch cayenne   juice or white wine
salt and pepper   vinegar
                                 2—4 oz. butter

1 Use a double saucepan if possible. If not a basin can be used. Put the egg yolks, seasonings and vinegar into the top of the pan, or basin.

2 Whisk over hot water until sauce begins to thicken.*
3 Add the butter in very small pieces, whisking in each pat until it has completely melted before adding the next. DO NOT ALLOW TO BOIL or it will curdle.
4 If too thick add a little cream.

    *Cooking time for this varies. If a double saucepan or large basin is used over hot water, the cooking will be quicker, but take special care that sauce does not curdle

Horseradish sauce

cooking time   8 minutes

you will need:

ingredients as white   2 tablespoons grated
    sauce (see page 91)   horseradish
1 dessertspoon vinegar   little cream
                                 pinch sugar

1 Make white sauce (see page 91).
2 Whisk in the vinegar and horseradish.
3 Add the cream and sugar.

Mexican sauce

no cooking

you will need:

2 large tomatoes   2 tablespoons olive oil
1 large onion   2 teaspoons Tabasco
2 tablespoons finely   sauce
    chopped parsley   ½ teaspoon salt

1 Chop tomatoes and onion finely, and add parsley.
2 Combine oil, Tabasco sauce and salt and mix with the chopped vegetables.
3 Serve with cold meats or cheese.

Mustard sauce

cooking time   8 minutes

you will need:

ingredients as for white   ½—1 teaspoon dry
    sauce (see page 91)   mustard
                             extra milk or cream

1 Blend the dry mustard with the flour.
2 Make the white sauce.
3 Stir in the extra milk or cream.

Onion sauce

cooking time   40 minutes

you will need:

8 oz. onion	1 oz. plain flour
water to cover	$\frac{1}{4}$ pint milk
1 teaspoon salt	seasoning to taste
1 oz. butter or margarine	

1 Cover onions with water, add salt and cook for 30 minutes or until tender.
2 Drain (reserving a $\frac{1}{4}$ pint liquor for the sauce) and chop onions finely.
3 Melt fat in a pan, add flour and cook without browning for 2 minutes.
4 Remove from heat, gradually add onion water and milk and reheat, stirring until sauce comes to the boil and thickens.
5 Add onions and simmer for 5 minutes.
6 Taste, season and pour into warmed sauceboat.

Parsley sauce

cooking time   8 minutes

you will need:

ingredients as for white sauce (see below)	1–2 teaspoons chopped parsley
	squeeze lemon juice

1 Make white sauce and add the chopped parsley.
2 Blend in the lemon juice.

Salad cream

cooking time   12 minutes

you will need:

1 tablespoon cornflour	seasoning
$\frac{1}{2}$ pint milk	1 teaspoon sugar
2 oz. butter or 2 tablespoons olive oil or corn oil	pinch dry mustard
	2 eggs
	$\frac{1}{4}$ pint vinegar

1 Blend cornflour with milk, put into a saucepan with butter or oil and plenty of seasoning and sugar.
2 Bring to the boil and cook until thickened.
3 Let it cool slightly, add beaten eggs and cook WITHOUT BOILING for several minutes.*
4 Cool again slightly, then whisk in the vinegar. Allow to get cold before using.

*If wished the cornflour mixture can be transferred to a double saucepan or basin over hot water so the eggs can be cooked with the sauce without fear of curdling

Tartare sauce

no cooking

you will need:

mayonnaise (see page 36)	2 teaspoons chopped capers
2 teaspoons chopped parsley	little chopped tarragon, if available or few drops tarragon vinegar
2 teaspoons chopped gherkins	

1 Make the mayonnaise and add chopped parsley, gherkins and capers.
2 If available add also a very little chopped tarragon or a few drops tarragon vinegar.

Tomato sauce

cooking time   40 minutes

you will need:

1 oz. butter	$\frac{1}{2}$ oz. flour or $\frac{1}{4}$ oz. cornflour
1 small onion	$\frac{1}{2}$ pint stock or liquid from canned tomatoes
1 carrot	good pinch salt, pepper and sugar
1 rasher bacon	
5 large fresh or canned tomatoes	
1 bay leaf	

1 Heat the butter and toss the diced onion, carrot and bacon in this—do not brown.
2 Add tomatoes and bay leaf and simmer.
3 Blend the flour with the stock, add to the ingredients and simmer gently for about 30 minutes, stirring from time to time.
4 Rub through a sieve, add seasoning and sugar and reheat.

White sauce

cooking time   8 minutes

you will need:

1 oz. butter or margarine	$\frac{1}{2}$ pint milk to give coating consistency, or $\frac{1}{4}$ pint milk to give panada or binding consistency, or 1 pint milk for thin sauce
1 oz. flour	
salt and peppers	

1 Heat the butter gently.
2 Remove from the heat and stir in the flour.
3 Return to the heat and cook gently for a few minutes without browning.
4 Again remove the pan from the heat and gradually blend in the cold milk.
5 Bring to the boil and cook, stirring with a wooden spoon, until smooth.
6 Season well.
7 If any small lumps have formed, whisk sharply.

INDEX